Miniature Perfume Bottles

Glinda Bowman

Schiffer Publishing Ltd

77 Lower Valley Road, Atglen, PA 19310

Dedication

This book is dedicated to everyone who enjoys beautiful things.

Published by Schiffer Publishing, Ltd.
77 Lower Valley Road
Atglen, PA 19310
Please write for a free catalog.
This book may be purchased from the publisher.
Please include $2.95 postage.
Try your bookstore first.

We are interested in hearing from authors
with book ideas on related subjects.

Printed in Hong Kong.
ISBN: 0-88740-628-9

Preface

The trend of collecting beautiful miniature perfume bottles is steadily increasing due to more availability on the market today. Miniature perfume bottles are usually exact replicas of the larger perfume bottles and contain the same quality fragrances, therefore making these tiny versions unique. Miniature perfume bottles are created by perfume companies to introduce and promote new fragrances to the perfume market. Most important, these miniature perfume bottles, empty or full, are collectibles and some may never be produced again. Take advantage now, while they are becoming more plentiful on the market and collecting is still relatively new. Naturally, the smaller perfume bottles are more affordable than full-sized bottles and less space is needed to display them, not forgetting the enjoyment and fun in acquiring such a unique collection.

I started collecting miniature perfume bottles over four years ago when my husband pointed out a few to me at a local flea market. I have been collecting them ever since, with a never-ending excitement about each different little bottle I find. I became intriqued by the size as well as by the bottle design and detail. I soon realized that this form of art was collectible, affordable, and available.

Since my husband enjoys helping me find new miniatures for my collection, we both go through the flea markets, with him looking down one aisle while I look down the other, so that we don't overlook a single one. We also look for them at garage sales, department stores, even while on vacation. It's like an obsession.

Discovering a different perfume bottle is like finding a precious treasure that you can't wait to take home, identify and clean before adding to the rest of the beautiful collection. These gorgeous little bottles look pretty whether displayed in a glass curio, on the shelves of a printer drawer or just sitting on a glass tray on your dresser. However you display them, they are beautiful.

After I acquired a sizeable collection, naturally I looked for a book on the subject of collecting miniature perfume bottles in order to identify my collection. Unfortunately, I could not find an informative book that featured a large quanity of the miniature perfume bottles, so I decided there was a need for this book. I am happy to share my collection with everyone in the hopes of encouraging others to start a collection and become part of this collecting trend.

Since I have become so involved in miniature perfume bottles, I have opened a shop, The Parfum Boutique, to sell and promote miniature perfumes. I am fortunate to have the opportunity to pursue my interests in miniature perfume bottles to such an extent and would enjoy hearing from other collectors. Please address all correspondence to: Glinda Bowman, 515 Fairmont Ave., Wheeling, WV 26003.

Writing this book has been a pleasure and I hope it encourages everyone to start collecting now.

Acknowledgements

I want to thank everyone who helped me in any way with their thoughts and ideas on this book:

Pat Bahr, Sherry Bahr, Zigy A. Blake, Michele Bowman, Sung Hye Davidson, Debbie Dearth, Elisa Dziatkowicz, Angela Feenerty, Letica Sanchez at Fragrance Plus, Susan Sanford, Monika Thompson, Lucille Valentine, and my husband John R. Bowman.

I am grateful to my publisher Peter Schiffer, my editor Leslie J. Bockol, and Doug Congdon-Martin, the professional photographer who took all the beautiful pictures.

Contents

Introduction

The use of fragrances has become an important part of our everyday lives, almost to the extent of becoming a necessity. Imagine a day without the fragrant scents we have in soap, deodorant, shampoo, household cleaners, air fresheners, and especially the fragrant perfumes we wear everyday. Life would be bland without fragrant scents to enhance the odors we smell.

Fragrances have become an accepted part of our individual habits, and we tend to take them for granted. A person's choice of fragrance is as personal as his or her choice of hairstyle or clothing. Fragrances smell different on each individual because of our body chemistries; each one of us gives off a different body scent, even identical twins. This is because the scent each of us gives off individually is not a single, pure scent, but a variety of multiple scents produced by individual body composition and body reaction to substances. Therefore, it is impossible to choose a fragrance because it smells pleasant on someone else.

It is difficult to describe a fragrance in words. A scent can only be described by comparing it with another smell, because scent impressions are subjective to individual interpretations. Someone else can suggest what you smell, but you may have a different interpretation.

Although the methods of using fragrances were quite different in ancient times, the interest in fragrances is just as strong today. Down through the centuries, flowers and herbs were important staples, treasured by anyone who could obtain them. They were used for medicinal purposes, cooking, cleansing, bathing, deodorizing, disinfecting, religious offerings, anointment, and even seduction, to mention a few uses. Before the bath system was invented, bathing and cleanliness was not a habit practiced as it is today. People used perfume to hide unpleasant body odors, pouring large quantities over their bodies to cleanse themselves. The same measure applied to the living quarters; sprinkling the contents with a fragrant scent freshened the room.

The perfume containers, or bottles as we know them, were exquisitely designed by fine craftsmen. They used the finest materials available, making perfume containers quite expensive, a luxury affordable only to the wealthy upper classes. True, poorer classes of people surely created fragrant scents and made containers to hold them, but none to compare to the great works of art designed by the skilled artisans. The methods of producing perfumes have changed remarkably since the perfume revolution in the last half of the 19th century, making perfume affordable for all classes of people today. New techniques in the distillation and new materials have promoted the perfume industry into a successful world-wide industry.

Most of the beautiful bottled fragrances bought in stores today are simply a mixture of a number of fragrant natural or synthetic substances dissolved in an alcohol base, with the exception of perfumes, which contain more of an oil base. But creating a new fragrance is not a simple process and involves the skills of many knowlegeable artisans. The first process in perfumery involves distillation: in order to extract the volatile oils from a mixture of compounds, whether natural or synthetic, perfume makers condense and collect the vapors produced as the mixture is heated. This process increases the concentration of the substance. The blended compounds of a fragrance are works of art, and the perfumer must put his skills to work in order to produce a new fragrance. The skilled perfumer must have knowledge of thousands of aromatic substances, understanding the odor value of each substance as well as the blending range of each. The perfumer plays an important role in the creation and outcome of each new fragrance.

The bottle designer has the task of creating an original bottle that compliments the fragrance and identifies the perfume house that designed the fragrance. Along the way, the fragrance is given a name. As you can see, creating a new fragrance can be a very complex task.

Today, we have access to many manufactured products, most of them connected in some way to fragrances, whether natural or synthetic, with perfume remaining as one of the most important products. How lucky we are, for we can enjoy beautiful perfumes in their uniquely designed bottles and choose from a vast selection at affordable prices. The sophisticated world of perfumery has captured the beauty of fragrances along with distinctively designed miniature bottles that are becoming part of a growing collection trend. Since the interest in collecting miniature perfume bottles is steadily increasing, this book is written in the hopes of being informative as well as enjoyable. I want to share my miniature perfume bottle collection with everyone interested, and encourage others to start a collection now and enjoy the pleasure of this beautiful form of art.

Perfume

Every society known to exist has used scents in one fashion or another. Since the use of fragrances is a tradition that has become part of our social culture today, it is interesting to note some of the early history of perfume.

The word "perfume" comes from Latin: *per* means "through," and "fume," from *fumus,* means "smoke"; the first scents were created from the burning of woods, gums, and barks obtained from trees. To early man, the scented smoke was a comforting mystery that also carried his prayers up to the gods.

There is evidence that the Egyptians were probably the first civilization to use perfumes on a large scale. Early records of perfumery in Egypt surfaced when unguent vases carved in alabaster from 3500 B.C. were discovered. Unguents were salves and ointments for soothing or healing. They were used in religious ceremonies, in the embalming ceremony for their dead, and in their private lives for personal use.

Incense was burned in the temples by Egyptian priests. The unguents and fragrant oils used for anointment in religious ceremonies were prepared and sold by the priests, making it possible that the Egyptian priests were the first retail perfumers. Cinnamon and nutmeg were popular ingredients, making the fragrances hot and spicy. There are many references to aromatic substances in the Bible and the Hebrews probably learned of their existence through the Egyptians.

Vast quanities of scents were used by the Egyptians in their mummification process, which only the rich and noble could afford, while the ordinary laborers were dumped into common pits without ceremony. Only the pharoahs and high officials received top quality embalming treatments. In the mummification process, the brain was pulled out through the nose, in whatever fashion their primitive instruments would allow. Next, the heart, liver, lungs, and intestines were cut out of the body and placed in containers with scented preservatives. The empty body cavities were filled with fragrant plants and herbs, then stitched back together. The body was then drained of any remaining blood and put in a bath of minerals to dehydrate. After the body dehydrated, it was rubbed dry, and cloth pads were inserted under the shrunken skin areas to reshape it. Finally, the corpse was wrapped in cloth bandages that were soaked with scented ointments. The Egyptians believed in life after death, so the dead were buried with all their personal possessions, including large quanities of perfumes. Some tombs even had a mummy lavatory installed within. Slaves and servants were buried in the tombs to care for their masters in the afterlife. On pre-arrangement, the attendants volunteered to poison themselves at their master's death so they could be buried beside him.

There is no doubt that the Egyptians were the forerunners in the use of perfumes. Because the Egyptian people favored cleanliness and believed that being clean was being close to the gods, they designed unique bath systems. It was popular to massage the body with fragrant oils and ointments after a fresh bath. Egyptian men favored a woman's clean, soft, and scented skin. The bath systems were an important and enjoyable part of Egyptian life. It is believed that the use of scent by the Egyptians was followed by the whole world.

Since Babylon was on a main trade route that crossed over from Asia, it became an international scent market, and Babylonian women had a large selection of perfumes. Babylon was the chief market for eastern perfumes, and their scents became world-famous. Most of the perfumes were oils or wines scented with flowers or gums, that were rubbed over the body. Perfume was also used to scent the breath; scented liquids were held in the mouth for a period of time before being expelled.

The Greeks believed perfume was of a divine origin at first, but quickly changed their beliefs when the personal use of perfume became fashionable and developed into a world of commerce. The scent market flourished as hundreds of perfumers set up shop in Athens and sold a wide variety of perfumes.

In imperial times, the Romans followed the Greek's love of scents; Rome had almost as many perfume shops as Athens. In the early days, the Romans anointed their bodies with pure olive oil, but later mixed the oils with various fragrant perfumes. The use of these perfumed oils caused the perfume industry to flourish, producing cheap perfumes for the poor as well as expensive perfumes for the rich. The Romans took recognition for the bath systems when they added flower petals to perfume their baths, thus becoming famous for the earlier Egyptian invention.

The rose became a favorite with the Romans and they used it to scent everything, from public baths and fountains to wines and love potions. Rose water was given for indigestion, rose medicine was used to treat illnesses, and there was even a rose pudding. However, the fall of the Roman Empire in 476 A.D. brought a change not only in power but in the perfume trade of Rome as well. The Byzantine empire, which enjoyed the fragrances of the east, became the new center of the scent trade.

Later, the Arabs discovered that the aroma of plants could be extracted and preserved through the process of distillation, and they took over the lead as perfumers of the world. Their process became the most important discovery in the world of perfume, for it made available all the perfumes we have today. Before distillation, fragrances had to be blended into a wine base or a messy oily base, with no method of preserving the true scent of flowers for a long-lasting effect. The Arabs chose their favorite flower, the rose, for the distillation experiment. The creation of rose water, loved by the Arabs, remains a favorite all over the world.

The discovery of distillation revolutionized the perfume trade in Europe as well. The true essence of a fragrance could be preserved in a lasting form that improved the quality of the perfume. European perfume manufacturers were busy reproducing traditional scents of the Middle East by the end of the twelvth century. This brought favorite scents, and perhaps some that had never been available before, straight to the local trade market. The perfumer could be more creative in the midst of this new discovery. Creating a new scent at this time must have been an exciting challenge. Two of the new fragrances that appeared in Europe, HUNGARY WATER and LAVENDER WATER, became very popular at that time. The perfume trend spread throughout Europe, knowing no end. Women had a larger selection of perfumes available than they had ever known before, and the perfumers worked hard to keep up with the increased demand. The perfume business continued to thrive in the sixteenth century, with Europe in the lead.

Fragrances have been popular with men throughout history; in fact, men have used fragrances as much as women during certain periods. At one time, scented baths were commonly used by both men and women. This all changed with the fall of the Roman Empire, after which anything "Roman" was discarded, including perfume and the Roman baths. In medieval times and the Middle Ages, bathing and personal cleanliness were not always practiced habits. Perfumes were used to conceal the odors of the unwashed body and a vast quanity of perfume was consumed on a large scale for cleansing. Sometimes as much as four liters of fragrance was poured over the body, in the belief that this cleansed the body. Although the cleansing practices of our ancestors are hard to comprehend, we must understand that the bath system was not widespread at that time. After the terrible years of the plague and disease, the seventeenth century brought a new way of thinking. People realized that cleanliness was important to good health. The bath system became a symbol of pleasure that promoted good health as well. A fashionable trend in personal hygiene revived the interest in perfume. Scents returned for both women and men.

The methods of reproducing perfume changed remarkably in the last half of the nineteenth century and the early part of the twentieth century, making perfumes an affordable luxury to all classes of people today. New techniques in distillation and new materials such as synthetics have promoted the perfume industry into a successful world-wide market.

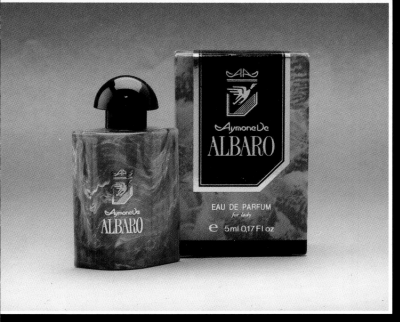

ALBARO eau de parfum for lady by Aymone De
Albaro, Italy. Distributed by Vapro International.
A plastic-encased 5ml .17oz. bottle.

MOSCHINO eau de toilette by Herp Alpert &
Co. Inc. Los Angeles, CA. The round bottle with
a gold stopper holds an oriental fragrance. 4ml
1/8oz.

LISTEN parfum by Herp Alpert & Co. Inc. Los
Angeles, CA. The fragrance that hits the perfect note, floral and fruity. 3.5ml .125oz.

ZEENAT eau de toilette by Zeenat Aman. Paris, France. The signature box contains a 7.5ml .25oz. bottle.

NEW WEST Skin Scent for her by Aramis. Los Angeles, CA. 7.5ml .25oz. The Saint Gobain Desjonqueres "S.D.G." trademark is on the bottle base.

DEVASTATING perfume by Anjou. NY, NY. 15ml 1/2oz.

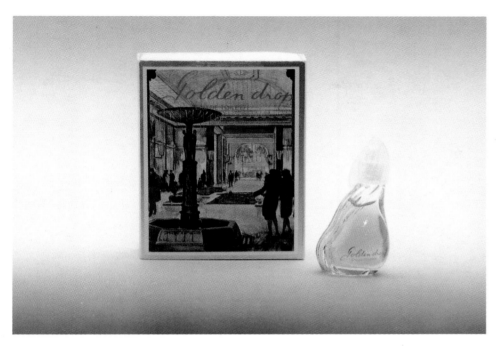

GOLDEN DROP eau de toilette by Arcad'Elysse. Paris, France. The small bottle looks like a golden droplet. 3.5ml 1/8oz.

BLUE GRASS Flower Mist by Elizabeth Arden Ltd. NY, NY. 15ml .5oz. Elizabeth Arden named her fragrance for the beautiful Kentucky blue grass.

RED DOOR eau de parfum by Elizabeth Arden Ltd. NY, NY. 7.5ml .25oz. A modern floral fragrance.

11

ARMANI eau de toilette by Parfums Giorgio Armani. Paris, France. Distributed by Cosmair, Inc. NY, NY. A floral blend fragrance. 5ml .16oz.

AMBERGRIS Oil by Alyssa Ashley. NY, NY. 14ml .48oz. The Ambergris oil comes from the sperm whale, which is no longer legally hunted for this purpose.

MUSK perfume by Alyssa Ashley. New York and France. 4ml .13oz. A scent for men or women.

DILYS eau de parfum by Laura Ashley Parfums. Paris, France. 3ml .1oz. The clear glass bottle holds a pinkish-colored fragrance.

HISTOIRE D'AMOUR parfum by Daniel Aubusson, Parfums. Paris, France. 4ml .14oz. The embossed glass bottle looks like a vase with an opaque flower for a stopper.

DANIEL De FASSON parfum deluxe pour femme by Daniel Aubusson. Made in Paris for Deco Distribution Group, Inc. Coconut Grove, FL. 3.7ml 1/8oz.

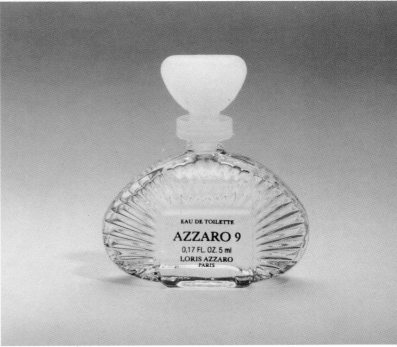

AZZARO 9 eau de toilette by Parfums Loris Azzaro S. A. Paris, France. 5ml .17oz. Distributed by The Wilkes Group, Inc. The Loris Azzaro bottle is a Dinand design.

SONATA parfum by J.S. Bach. Milan, Italy. 7.5ml .25oz. Distributed by Proteo.

LE DIX parfum by Balenciaga S. A. Paris, France. 3ml .1oz. The bottle has "HP" on its bottom, the trademark for Pochet et du Courval glassworks.

MICHELLE parfum by Balenciaga S. A. Paris, France. 5ml .16oz.

RUMBA eau de toilette by Balenciaga Inc. NY, NY, and Paris. 4ml .13oz. Distributed by The Fragrance Group, Ltd. A fluted clear glass bottle with an opaque stopper.

IVORIE de Balmain eau de toilette by Parfums Balmain. Paris, France. 7.5ml .25oz.

JOLIE MADAME parfum by Parfums Balmain. Paris, France. 1.8ml 1/16oz. The Saint Gobain Desjonqueres trademark "S" is on the base. The bottle is also used for other Balmain fragrances.

VENT VERT parfum by Parfums Balmain. Paris, France. 4ml .13oz. The Saint Gobain Desjonqueres trademark "S" is on the base of the bottle.

BASILE eau de parfum by Profumi Basile. Milan, Italy. 5ml .17oz. A feathered "B" is featured on the box and bottle.

LE BYOU NUIT perfume by Belafonte Int. New Haven, CT. 15ml 1/2oz. The frosted glass rose bottle sits on a square black base, which is the cap.

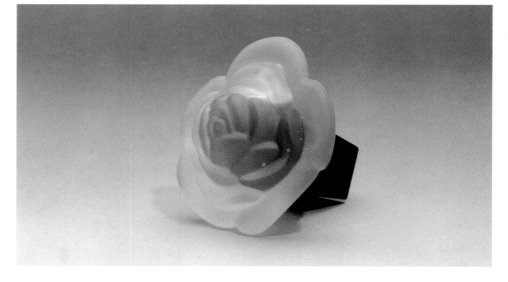

SKIN MUSK perfume oil by Bonnie Bell, Inc. Lakewood, OH. 3.7ml 1/8oz.

COLORS eau de toilette by Benetton Cosmetics Corp. Paris, France. 4ml .13oz. An oriental fragrance.

CHANSON D'AMOUR perfume by Jacques Bernier Inc. NY, NY. 15ml .5oz. A frosted heart is seen on the front of the bottle.

ROMA eau de toilette by Laura Biagiotti. Rome, Italy. 5ml .17oz. Distributed by Eurocos U.S.A., McFarlane and Associates. The Lorente-designed bottle represents an ancient Roman column. A very delicate pink toilette.

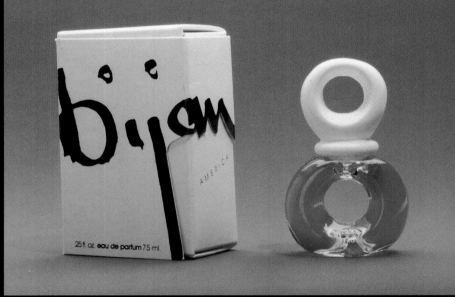

BIJAN eau de parfum by Bijan Fragrances, Inc. Beverly Hills, CA. 7.5ml .25oz. An oriental fragrance. The doughnut-shaped bottle comes in an unusual designed box.

TEMPORA parfum by A Blanc. 1.8ml 1/16oz.

EVENING STAR Parfum Traveler by Blanchard. NY, NY. 3.75ml 1/8oz. The bottle is encased in a gold shell with a rhinestone-encrusted gold top.

FLEUR de BOA eau de toilette by Parfums Boa. Paris, France. 7ml .23oz. The bottle is a design by Serge Mansau.

EVENING STAR, INTRIGUE, JEALOUSY, Parfums by Blanchard. NY, NY. 1.25 dram.

"A" ANDIAMO parfum by Princess Marcella
Borchese Inc. NY, NY. 7.5ml 1/4oz.

EVENING IN PARIS eau de toilette by Bourjois.
Distributed by Geo. W. Button Co. NY, NY.
.64 dram.

EVENING IN PARIS cologne, perfume, and
cologne, by Bourjois. NY, NY. .5 oz., .15oz.,
.25oz. All cobalt blue bottles.

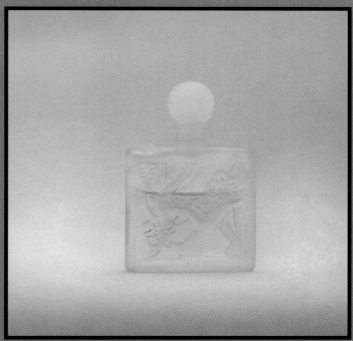

OMBRE BLEUE parfum by Jean-Charles Brosseau. Paris, France. Distributed by Alfin Inc. NY, NY.

EVENING IN PARIS perfume, eau de toilette by Bourjois. NY, NY. 1 dram, & .5oz. Both bottles are silver-plated.

OMBRE ROSE parfum by Jean-Charles Brosseau. Paris, France. Distributed by Alfin Inc. NY, NY. An oriental fragrance.

ANAIS ANAIS eau de toilette by Cacharel, Paris, France. Distributed by Cosmair, Inc. Annegrit Beier designed this bottle for Cacharel. The floral blend fragrance was named for Cacharel's

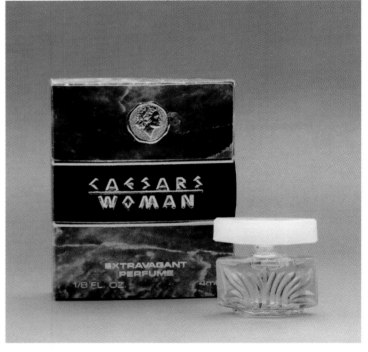

CAESARS WOMAN extravagant perfume by Caesars World Merchandising, Inc. Dist. Bev. Hills, L.A., CA. 4ml 1/8oz. From the pleasures of Caesars Palace.

LOU LOU eau de parfum by Parfums Cacharel. Paris, France. 5ml .17oz. Distributed by Cosmair, Inc. A floral blend fragrance. The hexagon shaped bottle is a design by Annegrit Beier.

CAFÉ parfum by Café Parfum. Paris, France.
4ml .13oz. Distributed by Fine Fragrances Inc.

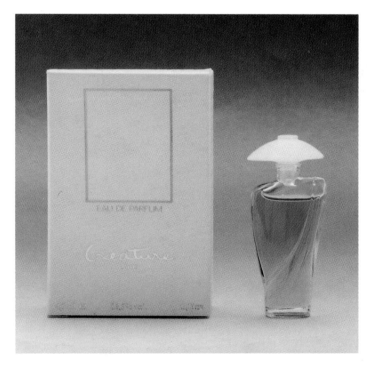

CREATURE eau de parfum by Parfums Giles
Cantuel. Paris, France. The tall Pochet et du
Courval bottle has an opaque white, mush-
room-shaped stopper. 4.5ml .15oz.

CAPUCCI eau de toilette by Parfums Capucci.
Distributed by Pardis Perfumes Inc. Paris,
France. The bottle has the Pochet et du Courval
trademark "HP" on the bottom. 5ml 1/6oz.

ROSE CARDIN eau de toilette is by Parfums Pierre Cardin. Paris, France. Distributed by Gary Farn, Ltd. Milford, CT. A beautiful rose-tinted bottle and black stopper. 7.5ml .25oz.

GRAFFITI parfum is by Parfums Capucci. Paris, France. 1.8ml 1/16oz.

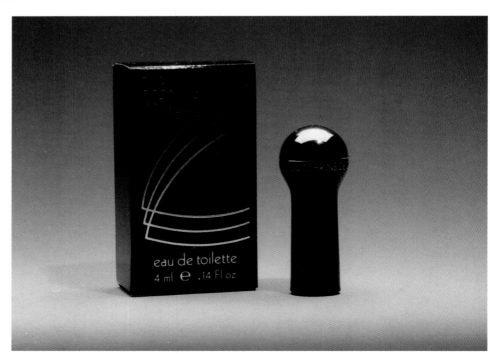

BLUE MARINE De Cardin eau de toilette by Parfums Pierre Cardin. Paris, France. 4ml .14oz. Distributed by Tsumura International.

BELLODGIA, FLEURS de ROCAILLE, NOC-TURNES, and TABAC BLOND parfums. A set by Caron. Paris, France. Distributed by Caron Corp. NY, NY. 7.5ml ,25oz.

INFINI perfume by Caron. Paris. Distributed by Caron Corp. NY, NY. 7.5ml 1/4oz.

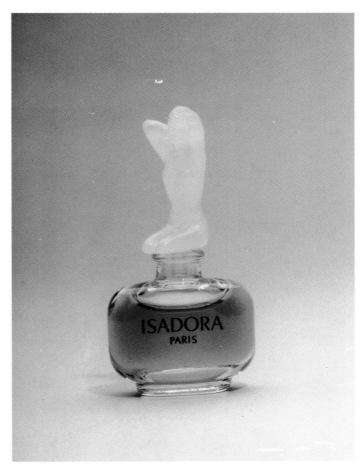

ISADORA parfum by Caron. Paris, France. The bottle has an opaque nude stopper. 3.75ml 1/8oz.

NOCTURNES parfum by Caron. Paris, France.
The bottle is black with a round clear stopper.
A modern floral fragrance. 7.5ml .25oz.

PARFUM SACRE eau de parfum by Parfums
Caron. Distributed by Jean Patou, Inc. Paris,
France. 3ml .1oz. Printed on the back of the
gold box is. "The very quintessence of rose.
Revealed by mystical spirit contained in a
flask, gilded in 24 carat gold."

NOCTURNES eau de toilette by Parfums Caron.
Distributed by Jean Patou, Inc. Paris France.
The clear glass bottle has the Pochet et du
Courval "HP" trademark on the bottom. 5ml
.16oz.

MUST de Cartier Parfum by Cartier, Inc. Paris, France. The gold-cased amber glass bottle holds an oriental fragrance. 4ml .13oz.

PANTHERE de Cartier parfum by Cartier, Inc. Paris, France. 4ml .13oz. A very beautiful Pochet et du Courval bottle.

FOREVER KRYSTLE perfume by Carrington Parfums Div. of Revlon Inc. NY, NY. 7.5ml .25oz. The crystal-cut, unmarked bottle came with a crystal pendant.

CASSINI eau de parfum by Oleg Cassini. Distributed by Cassini Parfums Ltd. NY, NY. The 4ml .125oz. bottle is made by Pochet et du Courval.

CHANEL No. 5 perfume by Chanel, Inc. Paris, France, and NY, NY. The famous "CHANEL No. 5" is a modern floral fragrance, the first sophisticated synthetic scent produced. The classic bottle was designed by Brosse. 10ml 1/3oz.

CHANEL No. 5 perfume by Chanel, Inc. Paris, France, and NY, NY. The 1/4 oz. bottle shown is probably the most popular size. CHANEL No. 5 is a subtle rather than sweet fragrance.

CHANEL No. 5 eau de toilette by Chanel, Inc. Paris, France. 7.5ml .25oz. In a much simpler bottle with a black label and a gold cap.

CHANEL No. 5 parfum by Chanel. Paris, France. 7.5ml 1/4oz. This square bottle with the round stopper is from a different period.

CHANEL No. 5 eau de toilette and eau de parfum by Chanel. Paris, France. 4.5ml .14oz. Two different shaped Chanel bottles with black caps.

CHANEL No. 19 eau de toilette by Chanel, Inc. Paris, France. Another of Chanel's numbered fragrances. 4.5ml .2oz.

CRISTALLE eau de toilette by Chanel, Inc. Paris, France. The 4.5ml .2oz. bottle comes in a blue velvet bag. A floral fruity fragrance.

COCO eau de toilette by Chanel, Inc. Paris, France. 4ml .13oz. The oriental fragrance bears the first name of the inimitable Chanel. Two differently shaped bottles are shown.

CRISTALLE eau de toilette by Chanel, Inc. Shown with its box. 4.5ml .2oz.

ENJOLI perfume by Charles of the Ritz Group Ltd. Div. of Revlon. NY, NY. 3.75ml 1/8oz.

BAVARDAGE parfum de Charieres. Paris, France. 1.8ml 1/16oz.

CHEVAL BLEU parfum by Charles V. Paris,
France. 1.8ml 1/16oz.

ENTENDU parfum by Charles V. Paris, France.
1.8ml 1/16oz.

CROYANCE parfum by Charles V. Paris,
France. 1.8ml 1/16oz.

MALICA parfum by Charles V. Paris, France.
1.8ml 1/16oz.

ORIENT parfum by Charrier. Paris, France.
1.8ml 1/16oz.

APRIL SHOWERS eau de toilette by Cheramy.
NY, NY. 3.75ml 1/8oz. This bottle was designed by Brosse.

VEUX TU parfum by Charrier. Paris, France.
1.8ml 1/16oz.

CASMIR eau de parfum by Parfums Chopard. Paris and Geneva. An oriental fragrance fills the Casmir bottle which has a red lotus blossom on its base. 5ml .17oz.

LIZ CLAIBORNE perfume by Liz Claiborne Cosmetics, Inc. NY, NY. 3.75ml 1/8oz. A floral blend fragrance.

DANGER parfum by Parfums Ciro. Paris, France. The round bottle, dressed in gold and a jewel, holds 1.25 drams.

REALITIES perfume by Liz Claiborne Cosmetics, Inc. NY, NY. The frosted glass bottle holds 5ml .17oz.

AROMATICS ELIXIR, Elixir Atomisaur Naturel by Clinique Laboratories, Inc. NY, London, and Paris. The frosted glass bottle holds a woody, aromatic fragrance.

NIKI de SAINT PHALLE parfum by Jacqueline Cochran. Paris, France. 6ml .20oz. Features two multi-colored, entwined serpents. The bottle is cobalt blue.

NIKI de SAINT PHALLE parfum bottle features two gold serpents on cobalt blue. 6ml .20oz.

4711 Original Eau De Cologne. Eau de Cologne and Parfumerie-Fabrik. Made at the street address of No. 4711 Glockengasse, Koln (Cologne), Germany. Approximately 1/8oz. The same blue and gold label has been used since the fragrance first appeared in 1792. "X 4711" is marked on the clear glass bottle's bottom. Distributed by Colonia, Inc.

NIKI de SAINT PHALLE parfum by Jacqueline Cochran. A 6ml .20oz., cobalt blue bottle. Distributed by Alfin Inc.

CAMP BEVERLY HILLS, The Splash by Colonia, Inc. Orange, CT. .15ml .5oz.

ELAN perfume concentrate by Coty, Inc. NY, NY. 15ml .5oz.

EMERAUDE and L'AIMANT parfums by Coty, Inc. NY, NY. The 4ml .13oz. bottles are encased in gold metal sleeves with bases of different colors and gold caps.

EMERAUDE perfume by Coty, Inc. NY, NY.
7.5ml .25oz.

EMERAUDE cologne by Coty, Div. of Pfizer.
NY, NY. This bottle of EMERAUDE is of a
different period. 7.5ml .25oz.

EMERAUDE perfume by Coty. 3.75ml .125oz.

LADY STETSON cologne by Coty, Div. of Pfizer.
NY, NY. 3/8oz.

L'ORIGAN eau de toilette by Coty. NY, NY. and
Paris, France. The 1.8oz. bottle has "COTY" in
raised letters on the bottom and the label is
embossed.

SAND & SABLE cologne by Coty, Div. of Pfizer.
NY, NY. 7.5ml .25oz.

Coty. This .25oz. bottle contained an unknown fragrance. COTY appears on the bottom of the bottle.

COURREGES IN BLUE eau de toilette by Courreges Parfums. Paris, France. Distributed by Jean Pax, Inc. The square patterned glass bottle has a gold stopper.

MONTAGE, RARE JEWEL, SILENT NIGHT toilette water. A set by Countess Maritza. NY, NY. 7.5ml .25oz.

CORIANDRE eau de toilette by Jean Couturier. Distributed by Classic Fragrances Ltd. Paris, France. 9ml .3oz.

SALVADOR DALI parfum and parfum de toilette by Parfums Salvador Dali. Paris, France. Distributed by Fine Fragrances Inc. Salvador Dali, the surrealist artist, designed his own bottle. The reproduction black bottle has a gold signature and "S. DALI" appearing on the bottom. The clear glass bottle contains parfum de toilette and shows off the lips and the opaque nose stopper. 5ml .17oz.

PLATINE parfum by Dana. Paris and New York. "DANA" appears on the bottom of the bottle and the word "PLATINO" on the other side of the label. 3.75ml 1/8oz.

TABU eau de parfum by Dana Perfumes Corp. NY, NY. 3ml 1/8oz.

TABU eau de toilette by Dana Perfumes Corp. NY, NY. The cello-shaped bottles have "DANA" on their bottoms. 7.5ml and 1/4oz.

LADY DI eau de toilette by Daver. Paris, France. The petite bottle has the Pochet et du Courval trademark and "FRANCE" on the bottom. 2ml 1/16oz.

OLIVIA perfume by Deborah International Beauty Ltd. NY, NY. 15ml .5oz.

DECADENCE parfum. Made in France for Deco Dist. Group, Inc. Coconut Grove, FL. 4.8ml .16oz.

ADOLFO eau de toilette by Adolfo Sardina, an American designer. Distributed by the Francis Denney Corp. Philadelphia, PA, and Trend Media Inc. 4ml .13oz.

ADOLFO cologne by Adolfo. Distributed by the Francis Denney Corp. Philadelphia, PA. 10ml .33oz.

"A" eau de toilette by Annabella. Distributed by R. P. Denis S. P. A. Milan, Italy. 5ml .17oz.

INTERLUDE parfum by Francis Denney. Distributed by Colonia, Inc. 3.75ml 1/8oz.

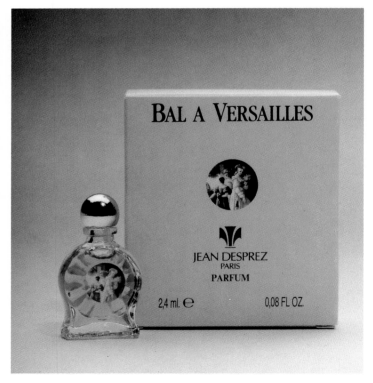

BAL A VERSAILLES parfum by Jean Desprez. Distributed by Alfin Inc. NY, NY. The 2.4ml .08oz. sunburst bottle has a picture of ladies at a Versailles ball.

BAL A VERSAILLES parfum by Jean Desprez. 2.4ml .08oz. This label is of an earlier period.

GIANFRANCO FERRE GFF eau de toilette by the designer of the same name. Diana De Silva Cosmetiques. Cormano, Italy. Distributed by Gary Farn, Ltd. Milford, CT. The 5ml 1/6oz. bottle contains a floral blend fragrance.

DIORESSENCE eau de toilette by Christian Dior Perfumes, Inc. Paris, France. 10ml .34oz. An oriental fragrance.

DIORISSIMO eau de toilette by Christian Dior Perfumes, Inc. Paris, France. 10ml .34oz. A floral blend fragrance.

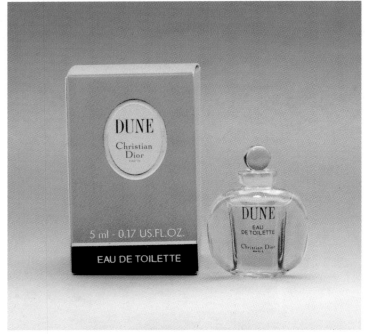

DUNE eau de toilette by Christian Dior Perfumes, Inc. Paris, France. 5ml .17oz.

MISS DIOR eau de toilette by Christian Dior Perfumes, Inc. Paris, France. 10ml .34oz. A chypre fragrance.

POISON esprit de parfum by Christian Dior Perfumes, Inc. Paris, France. Distributed from NY, NY. 5ml .17oz The dark purple bottle holds an oriental fragrance.

APPLE BLOSSOM perfume. Distributed by Duvinne. NY, NY. 3.75ml 1/8oz.

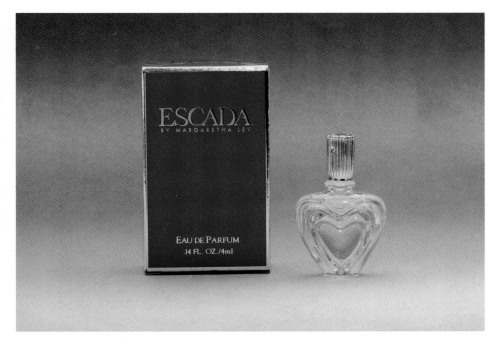

ESCADA eau de parfum by Margaretha Ley, Escada Beaute. Paris, France. 4ml .14oz. A floral oriental fragrance.

NAJ-OLEARI eau de toilette by Euroitalia SRL. Monza, Italy. The 5ml .16oz. frosted glass bottle appears to be cut in half. With an aqua green, cone-shaped stopper.

FABERGETTE WOODHUE perfume by Faberge. New York, and Paris, France. The tall slender bottle holds 1 dram 3.75ml.

TIGRESS perfume by Parfums Faberge. NY, NY. 7.5ml 1/4oz. The neck of the bottle has a gold-lettered "TIGRESS" tag tied to it. "Made in France" is on the bottom of the bottle.

LE JARDIN EXTRAIT eau de toilette and LE JARDIN FLEUR DE ROSE eau de cologne by Max Factor. Hollywood, CA. 3.5ml .12oz.

PROMESSE perfume by Max Factor. Hollywood, CA. 3ml .1oz.

GUESS eau de parfum by Fashion & Designer Frag. Group Inc. NY, NY. A Revlon Div. 3.5ml .12oz. An oriental fragrance by Georges Marcian.

LILY of the VALLEY and BRIGHT CARNATION
toilet water. Distributed by the Fuller Brush Co.
Hartford, CT. 1 dram.

TATIANA cologne spray by Diane Von
Furstenberg. Distributed by D.V.F. Inc. and
Revlon, Inc. NY, NY. A floral blend fragrance.

GALANOS parfum by James G. Galanos,
Parfums Galanos. Distributed by Gary Farn
Ltd. Milford, CT. 7.4ml .25oz.

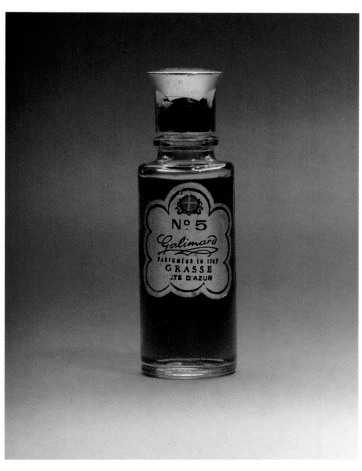

GALIMARO No. 5 parfum by Galimaro Parfumeur in 1747. Grasse, France. 15ml 1/2oz.

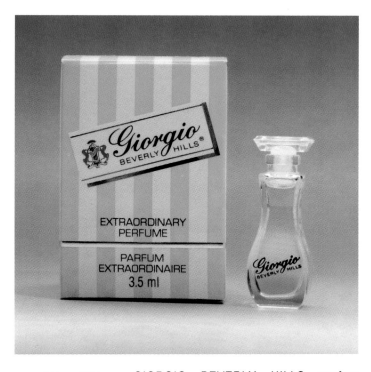

GIORGIO BEVERLY HILLS parfum extraordinaire, by Giorgio. Bev. Hills, CA. A floral blend fragrance. 3.5ml .11oz.

RED extraordinary perfume by Giorgio Beverly Hills. A woody aromatic fragrance. 3.5ml 1/8oz.

AMARIGE de GIVENCHY eau de toilette by Parfums Givenchy Inc. Paris, France. 4ml 1/8oz.

GIVENCHY III eau de toilette by Parfums Givenchy Inc. Paris, France. 4ml 1/8oz. A chypre fragrance.

EAU DE GIVENCHY eau de toilette by Parfums Givenchy Inc. Paris, France. 4ml 1/8oz.

L'INTERDIT eau de parfum by Parfums Givenchy Inc. Paris, France. 4ml 1/8oz. A modern floral fragrance.

YSATIS eau de toilette by Parfums Givenchy Inc. Paris, France. The 4ml 1/8oz. bottle was designed by Pierre Dinand. A floral oriental fragrance.

LE DE parfum by Parfums Givenchy Inc. Paris, France. 1.8ml 1/16oz.

CABOCHARD parfum by Parfums Gres. Paris, France. 1.8ml .06oz.

EAU de GUCCI parfum concentrate by Gucci. Paris, France. Distributed by Colonia, Inc. 7.5ml .25oz.

GUCCI PARFUM 1 by Gucci. Paris, France. 3.7ml 1/8oz.

GUCCI No. 1 eau de parfum by Gucci. Paris, France. Distributed by Scannon Ltd. NY, NY. 7.5ml .25oz.

GUCCI No. 3 parfum by Gucci. Paris, France. Distributed by Colonia, Inc. The 3.75ml 1/8oz. bottle contains a woody aromatic fragrance.

SAMSARA parfum by Guerlain. Paris, France. 2ml .07oz. The "HP" trademark is on the ruby glass bottle with gold trim.

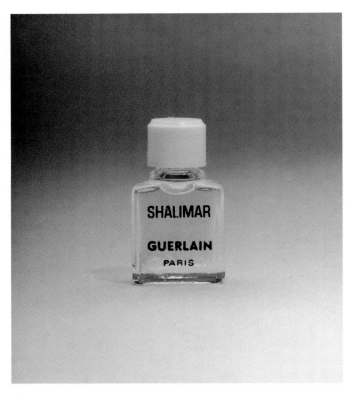

SHALIMAR parfum by Guerlain. Paris, France.
1.8ml 1/16oz.

SHALIMAR parfum by Guerlain. Paris, France.
Featuring the 2ml, 15ml, and 30ml classic crystal glass bottles and blue cut glass stoppers.
The design is by Raymond Guerlain and was
introduced to the U.S. in 1926.

SHALIMAR parfum by Guerlain. Paris, France.
The tiny 2ml .07oz. bottle comes in a velvet-
textured, deep lilac box.

56

HALSTON COUTURE perfume by Halston Fragrances Div. Distributed by Prestige Fragrances Ltd. NY, NY. The beautiful bottle has a silver plated stopper. 3.75ml 1/8oz.

273 by Fred Hayman Beverly Hills Exceptional Perfume. Distributed by the same. Beverly Hills, CA. 3.7ml 1/8oz. Fred Hayman's "273" perfume is his address on North Rodeo Drive. It is a floral blend fragrance.

...WITH LOVE perfume by Fred Hayman Beverly Hills. The 3.75ml 1/8oz. bottle is shaped in a parallelogram form.

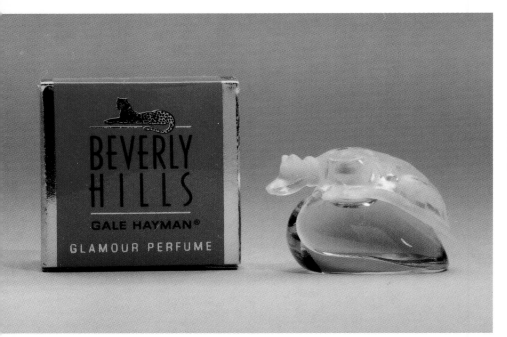

BEVERLY HILLS GLAMOUR PERFUME by Gale Hayman Beverly Hills. Beverly Hills, CA. The 3ml .1oz. sculptured bottle has an opaque spotted leopard stopper.

CALECHE eau de toilette by Hermes. Paris, France. 7.5ml 1/4oz. The bottle design is by Joel Desgrippes and holds a modern floral fragrance.

AMAZONE eau de parfum by Hermes. Paris, France. 7ml .23oz. A floral blend fragrance.

CIAO perfume by Houbigant. New York and Paris. 3.75ml 1/8oz.

HERMES eau de cologne by Hermes. Paris, France. 7.5ml .25oz. Beautiful translucent green bottle.

CAROLINA HERRERA eau de parfum by Carolina Herrera Perfumes. NY, NY. Distributed by Compar, Inc. 4ml .13oz. A floral blend fragrance. The box states, "Made in Spain by Antionio Puig S A Barcelona."

QUELQUES FLEURS L'ORIGINAL parfum by Parfums Houbigant. Paris, France. The 3ml .1oz. sculptured bottle comes in a lilac draw-string bag. "QUELQUES FLEURS" was one of the first successfully synthesized fragrances.

RAFFINEE parfum by Houbigant. Paris, France. Approximately 1/8oz.

RAFFINEE parfum by Houbigant. Paris, France. In a beautiful rose and gold 7ml .25oz. bottle.

HOUBIGANT gold case purse flacon holds approximately .25oz.

SKIN OIL. The bottle has Korean markings. Seoul, South Korea.

ICEBERG parfum by Iceberg Parfum, Eurocos. Funo, Italy. 4.5ml .17oz.

GARDENIA by Ivel. NY, NY. 7.5ml 1/4oz.

PARFUM RARE eau de toilette by Jacomo. Paris, France. 5ml 1/6oz. The Pochet et du Courval trademark is on the bottom of the bottle.

SILENCES parfum de toilette by Parfums Jacomo. Paris, France. 2.5ml 1/16oz.

JIL SANDER No. 4 eau de parfum by Jil Sander Cosmetics. Wiesbaden, Germany. 5ml .17oz.

JITROIS eau de toilette by Parfums Jean-Claude Jitrois. Paris, France. The green-tinted bottle looks like sculpted ice and has the "HP" Pochet et du Courval trademark on the bottom.

L'INSOLENT eau de parfum de Charles Jourdan. Paris, France. Distributed by Colonia, Inc. 3.75ml .125oz.

63

UN JOUR eau de toilette. Les Parfums Charles Jourdan. Paris, France. Distributed by Colonia, Inc. 2.5ml .08oz.

JOVAN MUSK perfume for women by Jovan Inc. Chicago, IL. Distributed by Quintessence Inc. 3.75ml 1/8oz.

"VOTRE" parfum de Charles Jourdan, Parfums S.A. Paris, France. Distributed by Colonia, Inc. 2ml 1/15oz. "CJ" is on the bottom of the bottle.

JOOP! eau de toilette by Parfums Joop! Paris, France, and Hamburg, Germany. "A name, a symbol, a man." 3.5ml .1oz. A floral blend fragrance.

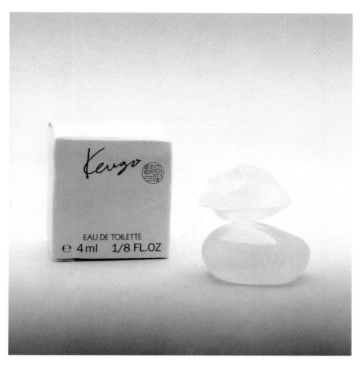

KENZO by Kenzo. Distributed by Tamaris S.A. Paris, France. 4ml 1/8oz. The squat, frosted glass bottle has a raised leaf design with an opaque, rose-shaped stopper.

ANNE KLEIN parfum by Parfums Anne Klein. Paris, France. Distributed by Parlux Ltd. 3.75ml 1/8oz.

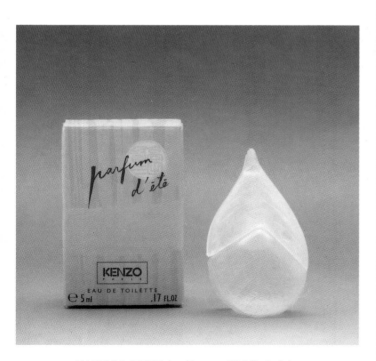

PARFUM D'ETE by Kenzo. Distributed by Tamaris S.A. Paris, France. 5ml .17oz. The frosted glass bottle looks like a leaf with a drop of water on it.

ANNE KLEIN II by Parfums Anne Klein. Paris, France. Distributed by Parlux Ltd. 3.75ml 1/8oz.

ESCAPE perfume by Calvin Klein Cosmetics Co. NY, NY. 4ml .13oz. A floral fruity fragrance that comes in a grey velvet bag.

OBSESSION perfume by Calvin Klein Cos. Co. NY, NY. An oriental fragrance. 3.5ml .12oz.

K de KRIZIA eau de parfum. Parma, Italy. Distributed by Sanofi Beauty Products. 4ml .13oz. The floral blend fragrance comes in a Dinand-designed bottle.

KRAZY KRIZIA eau de parfum. Parma, Italy. 6ml .2oz.

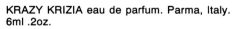

MOODS by KRIZIA eau de parfum. Parma, Italy. 6ml .2oz. Another Dinand-designed bottle for Krizia.

C'EST LA VIE! eau de parfum by Christian Lacroix Parfums. Paris, France. The 4ml .13oz. bottle with the coral stopper was designed by Maurice Roger.

TEATRO alla SCALA eau de parfum by Krizia. Parma, Italy. The modern floral fragrance is contained in a 3.75ml 1/8oz. bottle.

CHLOÉ eau de toilette by Lagerfeld. Distributed by Parfums Int. Ltd. NY, NY. 3.5ml .11oz. A floral blend fragrance.

ROYAL SECRET cologne spray by Lancaster Group. NY, NY. 7.5ml .25oz.

KL eau de toilette by Parfums Karl Lagerfeld. Paris, France. 10ml 1/3oz. The bottle design is by Marc Rosen and holds an oriental fragrance.

CHIYAT de LANCOME. Paris, France. 1.8ml 1/16oz. "Lancome" is on the bottom of the bottle.

MAGIE NOIRE eau de toilette by Lancome. Paris, France. An oriental fragrance. The 7.5ml .25oz. bottle was designed by Dinand.

TRESOR eau de parfum by Parfums Lancome. Paris, France. Distributed by Cosmair, Inc. NY, NY. TRESOR is a floral oriental fragrance and comes in a beautifully designed bottle by Areca. 7.5ml .25oz.

"O" de LANCOME eau de toilette by Lancome. Paris, France. The 7.5ml .25oz. bottle has the "S D G" trademark for Saint Gobain Desjonqueres on the bottom. Distributed by Cosmair, Inc. A chypre fragrance.

ARPEGE by Lanvin Parfums Inc. Distributed by Colonia, Inc. NY, NY. The 1/4oz. EAU ARPEGE bottle is shown with two gold-cased purse flacons from different periods. ARPEGE is a modern floral fragrance and was Lanvin's entry into the scent trade.

MY SIN extrait de Lanvin. Paris, France. Shown with the 1oz. bottle is a gold-cased purse flacon used for MY SIN and ARPEGE.

MY SIN parfum by Lanvin Parfums. Paris, France. 7.5ml .25oz. The bottle comes with a red cap in a clear plastic box.

CREATION parfum by Ted Lapidus. Paris, France. Distributed by The Fragrance Group Ltd. 4ml .13oz.

CLANDESTINE eau de toilette by Parfums Guy Laroche. Paris, France. 5ml .16oz.

FIDJI eau de toilette by Parfums Guy Laroche. Paris, France. Two bottles are shown. 1.8ml 1/16oz. and 5ml .16oz. The original bottle design was by Serge Mansau.

ALLIAGE eau d'alliage by Estee Lauder, Inc. NY, NY. 3ml .1oz. A chypre fragrance.

BEAUTIFUL perfume by Estee Lauder, Inc. NY, NY. The .12oz. bottle has no markings or label. BEAUTIFUL is a floral blend fragrance. The bottle was designed by I. Levy-Alan Carre.

j'aiOSE eau de toilette by Parfums Guy Laroche. Paris, France. Distributed by Parfums Beaute & Cie. Paris, France. 3.5ml .11oz.

KNOWING parfum by Estee Lauder, Inc. NY,
NY. .12oz. A chypre fragrance.

SPELLBOUND by Estee Lauder, Inc. NY, NY.
An oriental fragrance in a 3.7ml .12oz. bottle.

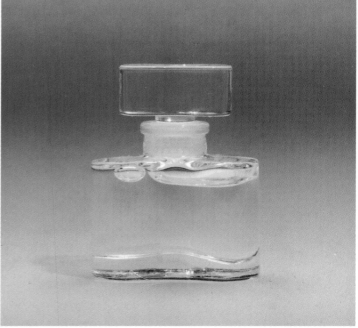

PRIVATE COLLECTION by Estee Lauder, Inc.
NY, NY. A chypre fragrance in a .09oz. bottle
marked "Made in France."

WHITE LINEN parfum by Estee Lauder, Inc.
NY, NY. A modern floral fragrance. .09oz.

YOUTH DEW by Estee Lauder was her first scent on the market. The two bottles, bath oil and eau de parfum spray in .25oz. bottles, contain an oriental fragrance.

MONOGRAM cologne by Ralph Lauren. Distributed by Warner Cos. of Cosmair Inc. NY, NY. A monogramed, cobalt blue bottle with silver shoulders and cap. 7.5ml 1/4oz.

LAUREN cologne by Ralph Lauren. Distributed by The Designer Fragrance Division, Cosmair Inc. NY, NY. 7ml 1/4oz. A floral bouquet blend fragrance.

SAFARI perfume by Ralph Lauren. Distributed by Cosmair, Inc. NY, NY. 4ml 1/8oz. A woody aromatic fragrance. "CPO" is on the bottom of the bottle.

SIROCCO cologne by Lucien Lelong. NY, NY. The 7.5ml .25oz. bottle is an original design by Lucien Lelong.

A'BIENTOT parfum by Lentheric. Paris, France. 4ml .13oz.

BALAHE eau de toilette by Leonard Parfums. Paris, France. 4ml 1/8oz. A beautiful black glass bottle.

VOICE eau de parfum by Christian de Lenclos. Paris, France. 5ml .17oz.

TAMANGO de LEONARD eau de toilette by Leonard Parfums. Distributed by Jean Pax, Inc. Paris, France. The 4ml Pochet et du Courval bottle has "LEONARD PARFUMS" on its bottom and was designed by Serge Mansau.

L de LOEWE eau de toilette by Loewe HNOS S.A.C. Madrid, Spain. Approximately 1/6oz.

BOB MACKIE parfums by Bob Mackie. Distributed by Rivera Concepts. Paris, France. The two versions of bubbled Pochet et du Courval bottles hold a floral blend fragrance. 4ml 1/8oz.

ONLY eau de toilette by Julio Inglesias. Distributed by MAS Cosmetics S.A. Barcelona, Spain. Distributed by Colonia, Inc. 10ml .3oz.

MAXIM'S DE PARIS parfum by Maxim's. Paris, France. Distributed by Gary Farn Ltd. Milford, CT. 4.5ml .14oz.

MCM eau de parfum by MCM Cosmetic. Munchen, Germany. 5ml .17oz.

MAXIM'S DE PARIS parfum by Maxim's. Paris, France. 10ml 1/3oz.

JMC perfume by Jessica McClintock. San Francisco, CA. 7.5ml 1/4oz.

DESTINY perfume by Marilyn Miglin Inc.
Chicago, IL. U.S. 3.75ml 1/8oz.

"BOUQUET" parfum by Melillo Studios. NY,
NY. 4ml .13oz.

MISSONI parfum by Missoni Profumi. Paris,
Milan, and NY. A chypre fragrance. Approximately 1/8oz.

CONCRETA parfum by Parfums Molinard. Grasse, France. 1 dram.

MOLINARD de MOLINARD eau de toilette. Paris, Grasse, France. Distributed by Gary Farn Ltd. Milford, CT. 7.5ml 1/4oz. A floral blend fragrance. This bottle is identical to the HABANITA bottle except in color. They have the same "Molinard Creation Lalique" on the bottom with the added "HP" trademark.

HABANITA de MOLINARD eau de toilette. Paris, Grasse, France. 7.5ml 1/4oz. An oriental fragrance. The original bottle was a René Lalique creation for Molinard. "Molinard Creation Lalique" is on the bottom of the bottle.

MON CLASSIQUE de MORABITO eau de toilette by Morabito Parfums. Paris, France. 7.5ml 1/8oz.

OR NOIR eau de toilette by Pascal Morabito Parfums. Paris, France. 4ml 1/7oz.

MAJA eau de toilette by Myrugia. Barcelona, Spain. Distributed by Colonia, Inc. Approximately .25oz.

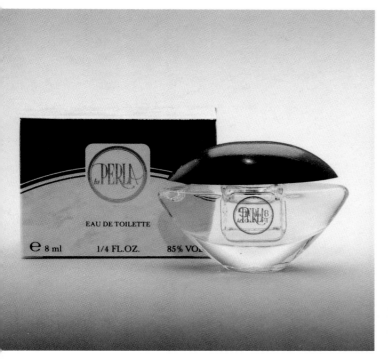

LaPERLA eau de toilette. Distributed by Morris. Italy. 8ml 1/4oz.

BOTANICAL, SEA SPLASH, and TROPICS colognes by Naturalistics. Del Labs. Farmingdale, NY. In 4.9ml .17oz. frosted bottles.

ALBERT NIPON perfume by Albert Nipon Fragrance Inc. NY, NY. 3.7ml 1/8oz. The bottle has no label or markings.

INCOGNITO perfumed cologne by Cover Girl, Noxell Corp. Hunt Valley, MD. The frosted glass bottle has a green, marbled stopper. 3ml .1oz.

NAVY cologne by Cover Girl, Noxell Corp. Hunt Valley, MD. 3ml .1oz.

FLEURS D'ORLANE eau de toilette by Orlane.
Paris, France. 5ml .16oz. Secret De Parfum.

OMAR SHARIF pour femme eau de toilette
by Parfums Omar Sharif. Paris, France.
The Pochet et du Courval bottle holds
7.5ml 1/4oz.

RUFFLES espirit de parfum by Oscar De La
Renta. Distributed by Parfums/Paris. Paris,
France. 4ml .13oz. A floral blend fragrance.

CALANDRE eau de calandre by Paco Rabanne. Paris, France. Distributed by Compar, Inc. A modern floral fragrance contained in a 5ml .17oz. bottle.

METAL eau de metal by Paco Rabanne. Paris, France. Distributed by Compar, Inc. The 5ml .17oz. Pochet et du Courval bottle contains a chypre fragrance.

LA NUIT eau de parfum by Paco Rabanne. Paris, France. 5ml .17oz. The "S G D" trademark of Saint Gobain Desjonqueres is on the bottle base.

SWANN eau de toilette by Pacoma Parfumer. Distributed by J. Pax Inc. Miami, FL. The 4ml 1/8oz. bottle has "PACOMA" and "PARIS" on the base.

CHLOE NARCISSE parfum by Parfums Int. Ltd. NY, NY. 3.75ml 1/8oz.

WHITE DIAMONDS parfum by Elizabeth Taylor and Parfums Int. Ltd. NY, NY. 3.75ml 1/8oz. A woody, aromatic fragrance.

PASSION parfum by Elizabeth Taylor and Parfums Int. Ltd. NY, NY. 3ml 1/8oz.

WHITE SHOLDERS parfum by Parfums Int. Ltd. NY, NY. A floral blend fragrance. 7.5ml .25oz.

CHANTILLY perfume by Parfums Parquet. NY,
NY, and Paris, France. 3.5ml .12oz.

PRESENSE fragrance by Parfums Parquet.
NY, NY, and Paris, France. 3.5ml .12oz.

LUTECE perfume by Parfums Parquet. NY,
NY, and Paris, France. 3.5ml .12oz.

No. 3 PARK & TILFORD fragrance. NY, NY.
3ml .1oz.

SPECTACULAR perfume by Joan Collins and Parlux Ltd. Paris, France. 5ml .17oz.

ANIMALE eau de parfum by Parlux Fragrances Inc. U.S.A. Distributed by Parlux S.A. Paris, France. 5ml .17oz.

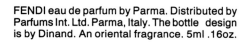

FENDI eau de parfum by Parma. Distributed by Parfums Int. Ltd. Parma, Italy. The bottle design is by Dinand. An oriental fragrance. 5ml .16oz.

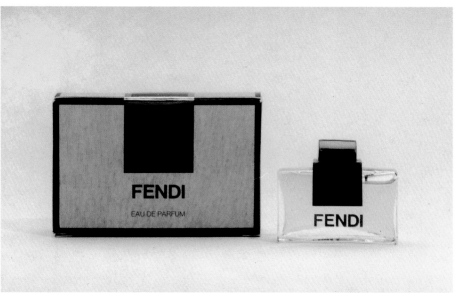

JOY eau de toilette by Jean Patou, Inc. Paris, France. 2ml .07oz. The floral blend fragrance was at one time marketed as the most expensive parfum in the world. The original bottle design was by Louis Sue. The "JP" monogram is on the bottle cap.

MA LIBERTE eau de toilette De Jean Patou, Inc. Paris, France. 3ml .2oz. "Jean Patou, Made in France" is on the base of the bottle and the "JP" monogram is on the back.

'1000' eau de toilette by Jean Patou, Inc. Paris, France. 2ml .07oz. "Jean Patou Bot. Made in France" on the bottom of the bottle.

PAVLOVA 1922 parfum by Parfums Payot. Distributed by Colonia, Inc. Paris, France. 2ml .06oz. The fragrance was named for Anna Pavlova, a ballerina of the "Revue Russe."

SAMBA perfume by The Perfumers Workshop Ltd. NY, NY. 3.75ml 1/4oz. "SAMBA" is on the bottom of the bottle.

TEA ROSE parfum by the Perfumers Workshop Ltd. NY, NY. The fragrance comes in a crystal, rose-shaped, opaque pink bottle. 15ml 1/2oz.

TEA ROSE parfum by The Perfumers Workshop Ltd. NY, NY. 5ml 1/6oz. An oriental fragrance.

PALOMA PICASSO eau de parfum spray by Parfums Paloma Picasso. Paris, France. Distributed by Cosmair, Inc. NY, NY. "PALOMA PICASSO" is etched on the gold case, and the fragrance comes with a red velvet autographed slip on cover. A chypre fragrance.

PALOMA PICASSO eau de parfum by
Parfums Paloma Picasso. Paris, France.
The chypre fragrance comes in a bottle
designed by Paloma, daughter of Pablo Picasso.
Approximately 1/8oz.

BANDIT parfum by Robert Piguet. Paris, France.
4ml .13oz. Distributed by Alfin, Inc. NY, NY.

BAGHARI parfum by Robert Piguet. Paris,
France. 1.8ml 1/16oz.

FRACAS parfum by Robert Piguet. Paris,
France. 4ml .13oz. Distributed by Alfin, Inc. NY,
NY. A floral bouquet blend fragrance.

CALYX perfume spray by Prescriptives. NY, NY. 5ml .18oz. The frosted glass bottle contains a floral fruity fragrance.

VISA parfum de Robert Piguet. Paris, France. A 4/5 dram bottle in plaid and gold.

MONTANA eau de toilette by Montana Parfums and Prestige Fragrances Ltd. NY and France. A miniature of the bottle designed by Serge Mansau. 2ml .07oz.

NORELL perfume by Prestige Fragrances Ltd. NY, NY. 3.75ml 1/8oz. A floral blend fragrance.

MOMENTS parfum splash by Priscilla Presley. Orange, CT. Distributed by Muelhens Inc. 2.4ml .08oz.

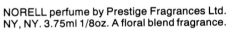

SCAASI eau de parfum by Prestige Fragrances Ltd. NY, NY. 3.75ml 1/8oz.

AVIANCE NIGHT MUSK perfume oil by Prince Matchabelli. NY, NY. 7.5ml .25oz.

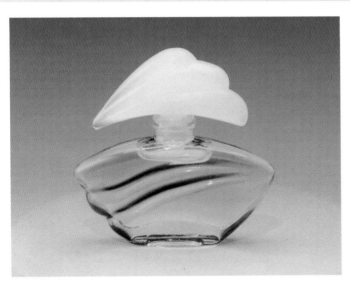

ADDED ATTRACTION perfume by Prince Matchabelli. NY, NY. The 1 dram bottle is a beautiful rendition of the Matchabelli crown.

LUNA MYSTIQUE eau de parfum by Prince Matchabelli, Inc. Greenwich, CT. 7.5ml .25oz.

BELOVED creme sachet perfume 1oz., GOLDEN AUTUMN perfume .5 dram, PROPH-ECY perfume 1 dram. All by Prince Matchabelli. NY, NY.

WIND SONG perfume by Prince Matchabelli, Inc. Greenwich, CT. 7.5ml .25oz.

VIVARA parfum by Emilio Pucci. Paris, France. 1.8ml 1/16oz. The bottle has "France" and the "HP" trademark on the bottom.

JACLYN SMITH'S CALIFORNIA eau de cologne. Manufactured by Procter & Gamble Cosmetics & Fragrance Products. 7ml .3oz.

ASPEN cologne spray for women by Quintessence Inc. Chicago, IL. 11.1ml 3/8oz.

REPLIQUE parfum by Raphael. Paris, France.
1.8ml 1/16oz.

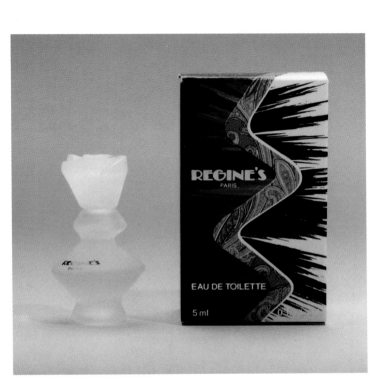

REGINE'S eau de toilette by Parfums Regine's.
Paris, France. 5ml .17oz.

DETCHEMA parfum by Parfums Revillon. Paris,
France. Approximately 1/8oz. A Pochet et du
Corval bottle.

INTIMATE perfume by Revlon, Inc. NY, NY. 3ml .1oz. Purse flacon.

JONTUE perfume by Revlon, Inc. NY, NY. 6ml .2oz. A beautiful bottle with a tag label.

MAROC ULTIMA II parfum atomiseur by Revlon, Inc. NY, NY. 10ml 1/3oz.

INTIMATE perfume by Revlon, Inc. NY, NY. 7.5ml .25oz.

BILL BLASS perfume replica by Charles Revson, Inc. NY, NY. 3.75ml 1/8oz.

SCOUNDREL cologne spray by Revlon, Inc. NY, NY. 7.5ml .3oz.

BASIC BLACK, black cap, HOT, red cap, NUDE, white cap, a set of three perfume replicas by Charles Revson, Inc. NY, NY. 3.75ml 1/8oz.

CIARA perfume by Charles Revson. NY, NY.
3.75ml 1/8oz.

"L'AIR du TEMPS" eau de toilette by Nina Ricci.
Paris, France. 3.75ml 1/9oz. The beautiful bottle
is based on a Marc Lalique design. Nina Ricci
created the fragrance in 1947.

MAROC espirit de parfum by Charles Revson.
NY, NY. 3.75ml 1/8oz.

L'AIR du TEMPS eau de toilette by Nina Ricci.
Shown is the Romantic Flacon alone and in the
plastic dome. Designed by Marc Lalique, the
bottle with the stopper of two touching doves in
flight contains a floral blend fragrance.

L'AIR du TEMPS eau de parfum by Nina Ricci. The Dove Flacon is a Lalique creation. 3.5ml .11oz.

"L'AIR du TEMPS" parfum by Nina Ricci. This is the .17oz. Purse Dove Lalique Flacon.

L'AIR du TEMPS parfum by Nina Ricci. The braided gold wire Opera Flacon with a gold dove cap comes with a gold funnel or 'cheminee' in a brown velvet case. The .17oz. bottle is marked with "Nina Ricci, Made in France" on the bottom.

"L'AIR du TEMPS" eau de parfum by Nina Ricci. The Opera Flacon by Lalique has "Made in France" on the bottom. .17oz.

MADEMOISELLE RICCI eau de toilette by Nina Ricci. Paris, France. 5ml .16oz. A Lalique creation.

BYBLOS eau de parfum by Rivara Div., Hanorah S.P.A. Milan, Italy. The cobalt blue bottle holds 7.5ml .25oz. and is topped with a gold rose stopper.

NINA eau de toilette spray by Nina Ricci. Paris, France. .14ml 1/2oz.

GENNY eau de toilette by Rivara Div., Hanorah S.P.A. Milan, Italy. 5ml .17oz. The "S G D" trademark is on the bottom of the bottle.

BYZNACE eau de parfum by Rochas, distributed by Jean Patou, Inc. Paris, France, 3ml .1oz. The beautiful blue bottle contains a modern floral fragrance.

LUMIERE eau de parfum by Rochas, distributed by Jean Patou, Inc. Paris, France. The 3ml .1oz bottle is a beautiful opaque blue with a mauve, diamond-cut stopper.

FEMME eau de parfum by Rochas, distributed by Jean Patou, Inc. Paris, France. The chypre fragrance comes in the 3ml .1oz Saint Gobain Desjonqueres bottle.

MACASSAR eau de toilette by Parfums Rochas. Paris, France. 5ml .17oz.

ROMEO eau de parfum de Romeo Gigli. Milan, Italy. 7.5ml .25oz. The stylist, Romeo Gigli, has a floral fruity fragrance.

MADAME ROCHAS parfum de toilette by Rochas., distributed by Jean Patou, Inc. The "S G D" bottle contains a modern floral fragrance. 3ml .1oz.

PRIVILEGE parfum by Edmond Rosens. Paris, France. 4ml .13oz. The bottle has no label.

TITA parfum de Tita Rossi. Paris, France. The flacon miniature holds 5ml .17oz.

SOCIETY by Burberrys. Royal Brands International. Distributed from NY, Switzerland, and London. There is no label on the slender fluted glass bottle. The opaque brown stopper has a silver knight stamped on it. A floral blend fragrance is contained in the 4ml .14oz. bottle.

C'EST parfum by Royal Ungary. Paris, France. 1.8ml 1/16oz.

MAI TAI perfume by Royal Hawaiian Perfume, Ltd. Honolulu, Hawaii. 15ml 1/2oz.

PARADIS perfume by Saks Fifth Avenue. U.S.A. 7.5ml .25oz. A floral fruity fragrance.

SCHERRER 2 eau de parfum by Parfums Jean-Louis Scherrer. Paris, France. Distributed by Parfums International. Ltd. NY, NY. 3.7ml 1/8oz.

SINAN de J. Marc Sinan parfum. Paris, France. Approximately 1/8oz. The stopper is shaped like a rib.

SHOCKING parfum by Schiaparelli. Paris, France. 4ml .13oz. The original bottle design was by Elsa Schiaparelli. The bottle is shaped like a dressmakers' form.

SINAN de Jean-Marc Sinan eau de toilette. 5ml .16oz. The two bottles differ in the stoppers. Most appear like the one on the right. However, some variations can exist.

DENEUVE eau de toilette by Catherine Deneuve. Paris, France. Distributed by Parfums Stern and Sanofi Beauty Products. The Pochet et du Courval bottle has a swirled sash stopper and contains a chypre fragrance. 4ml 1/8oz.

PERRY ELLIS perfume by Perry Ellis. Distributed by Parfums Stern and Sanofi Beauty Products. NY, NY. 4ml .14oz.

OSCAR de la RENTA parfum and eau de toilette. Distributed by Parfums Stern Inc. NY, NY. The bottle design is by Oscar de la Renta and the fragrance is a floral oriental. The bottle on the left holds perfume and is a little darker than the eau de toilette which has a frosted stopper.

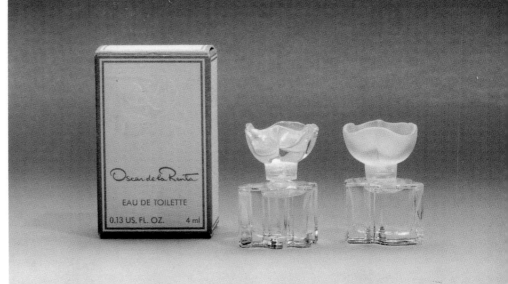

CHER UNINHIBITED perfume. Distributed by Parfums Stern, Inc. NY, NY. 3.7ml 1/8oz. The frosted stopper appears to be a quarter moon with moon beams and stars.

RUFFLES eau de toilette by Oscar de la Renta. Distributed by Parfums Stern Inc. NY, NY. The 5ml .17oz. bottle has no base.

CHER UNINHIBITED eau de toilette. Distributed by Parfums Stern, Inc. NY, NY. 10ml 1/3oz. The stopper in this case is silver and the box is shaped different.

VALENTINO eau de toilette by Valentino. Distributed by Parfums Stern Inc. Paris, France. Approximately 1/4oz. No label or markings on the bottle.

VOLUPTE parfum by Oscar de la Renta. Distributed by Parfums Stern Inc. and Sanofi Beaute Inc. NY, NY. The 4ml 1/8oz. bottle has a jewel green & gold stopper.

SUNG eau de toilette by Alfred Sung. Distributed by Rivera Concepts of America, Inc. The 4ml .14oz. bottle is a Pochet et du Courval in squares with no label.

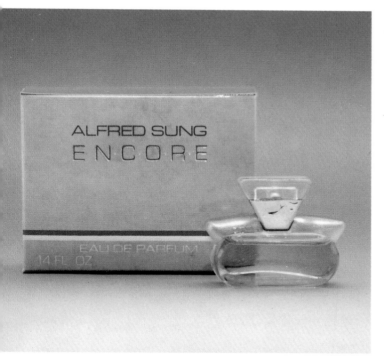

ENCORE eau de parfum by Alfred Sung. Distributed by Rivera Concepts of America, Inc. Beverly Hills, CA. 4ml .14oz. The bottle has the "HP" trademark on the bottom.

ORANGE BLOSSOM perfume by Howard Tawes. Miami, FL. 7.5ml 1/2oz. The bottle is attached to the base.

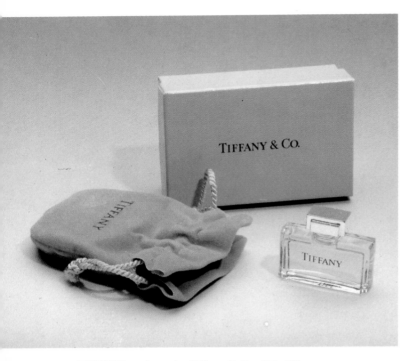

TIFFANY perfume by Tiffany & Co. NY, NY.
3.75ml 1/8oz. The bottle contains a floral oriental fragrance, and comes in a blue Tiffany bag.

BOUCHERON eau de parfum by Ultra Cosmetics. Paris and Geneva. 5ml .17oz. The bottle
has the "HP" trademark.

ACTION eau de toilette by Trussardi Parfums
S.P.A. Milan, Italy. The glass bottle is in a
plastic case.

DIVA eau de parfum by Parfums Ungaro. Paris,
France. 4.5ml .14oz. A chypre fragrance in a
Pochet et du Courval bottle. "UNGARO" is on
the bottom of the bottle.

SENSO eau de parfum by Emanuel Ungaro.
Paris, France. The bottle design is by Jacques
Helleu. 3ml .1oz.

UNGARO eau de parfum by Ungaro. Paris,
France. The cobalt blue bottle is 3ml .1oz.
Again by Jacques Helleu.

FIRST eau de toilette de Van Cleef & Arpels.
Distributed by Sanofi Beauty Products. Paris,
France. 5ml .17oz.

GEM eau de toilette de Van Cleef & Arpels.
Paris, France. A modern floral fragrance in a
5ml .17oz. bottle.

GLORIOUS perfume by Gloria Vanderbilt. Distributed by Cosmair, Inc. NY, NY. 4ml .13oz. A modern floral fragrance. No label or markings.

MOON SONG cologne by Vanda Beauty Consultant. 4ml .13oz.

VANDERBILT eau de toilette by Gloria Vanderbilt. Distributed by Cosmair, Inc. NY, NY. The two bottles have different caps, one gold, one silver. 7ml .22oz.

ECHO eau de parfum by Mario Valentino. Milan, Italy. Distributed by Fox Fragrances, U.S.A. 5ml .17oz.

VANDERBILT perfume by Gloria Vanderbilt. Distributed by Cosmair, Inc. NY, NY. 3.75ml 1/8oz. The original bottle design was by Bernard Kotyuk.

VENDETTA eau de toilette by Valentino. Milan, Italy. Distributed by Parfums International, Ltd. NY, London, Paris, Milan, Wien. 7.5ml .25oz.

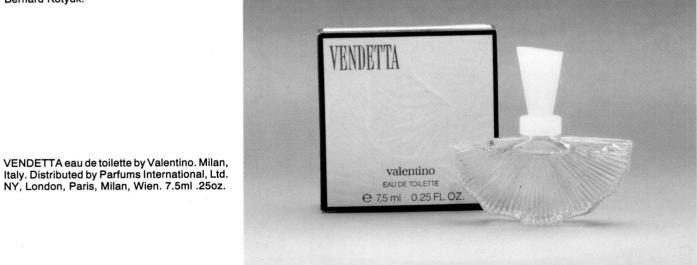

GIANNI VERSACE eau de toilette by Versace Profumi. Milan, Italy. 3.5ml 1/8oz. A chypre fragrance.

MAISSA eau de parfum by Jean Louis VermeiL. Paris, France. 7ml .23oz.

VE VERSACE eau de parfum by Versace Profumi. Milan, Italy. Distributed by Vepro U.S.A., Ltd. The 3.5ml 1/8oz. bottle contains a woody aromatic fragrance and was designed by Pierre Dinand.

PIQUETTE perfume by Pierre Vivion. NY, NY.
15ml 1/2oz.

SECRET de VENUS ZIBELINE. A bath and
body fragrance oil by Weil, Classic Fragrances,
Ltd. Paris, France. 7ml .22oz. The bottle has
"Made in France, Weil" on its bottom and is a
Pochet et du Courval.

ANTILOPE parfum by WeiL. Paris, France.
3.75ml 1/8oz.

WEIL de WEIL parfum by Weil, Classic
Fragrances, Ltd. Paris, France. 3.5ml 1/8oz.

DANS LA NUIT eau de toilette by Worth. Paris, France. 7ml .22oz. The cobalt blue bottle has "WORTH" on the front and the fragrance name on the stopper. The bottle is a design by Lalique.

GILDA eau de toilette by Pierre Wulff. Paris, France. Approximately 1/6oz.

JE REVIENS parfum by Parfums Worth. Paris, France. The 3.75ml 1/8oz. bottle contains a floral blend fragrance and the original cobalt blue bottle was designed by René Lalique.

OPIUM eau de toilette by Yves Saint Laurent Parfums Corp. Paris, France. 3.5ml .1oz. An oriental fragrance.

PARIS parfum and eau de toilette by Yves Saint Laurent Parfums Corp. Paris, France. 7.5ml .26oz. The parfum has the gold stopper.

RIVE GAUCHE eau de toilette by Yves Saint Laurent Parfums Corp. Paris, France. 3ml .1oz.

"Y" eau de toilette by Yves Saint Laurent Parfums Corp. Paris, France. The two bottles are a little different in their design and lettering. 7.5ml .26oz.

"Y" parfum by Yves Saint Laurent Parfums Corp. Paris, France. 4ml .13oz. The "Y" label is on the bottom of the bottle.

OMAR perfume by 667 Perfumes Inc. NY, NY. 7.5ml 1/4oz.

ZIG ZAG parfum by Zsa Zsa. Distributed from NY, NY. 7.5ml 1/4oz.

ADOLFO CLASSIC GENTLEMEN eau de toilette for men by Adolfo Fragrances, Inc. Paris, France. 15ml 1/2oz.

JAGUAR eau de toilette for men. Distributed by Alfin, Inc. Under license of Jaguar Cars Ltd. UK, and Zurich, Switzerland. A 5ml .17oz green bottle with a wooden cap.

ARMANI eau pour homme by Parfums Giorgio Armani. Paris, France. Distributed by Cosmair, Inc. NY, NY. "G Armani bottle made in Italy" is on the bottom of the bottle. The bottle is a Dinand design. The classic citrus fragrance comes in a 10ml .33oz. bottle.

TUSCANY eau de toilette for men by Aramis, Inc. NY, NY. 8ml .25oz.

AZZARO pour homme by Loris Azzaro. Distributed by The Wilkes Group, Inc. Paris, France. 7ml .24oz. A chypre fragrance.

COLORS eau de toilette de Benetton Cosmetics, Inc. Paris, France. 4ml .13oz. The bottle has "Benetton" on its bottom.

BOSS SPORT by Hugo Boss eau de toilette. Frankfurt, Germany. Distributed by Eurocos U.S.A., Macfarlane & Associates. 5ml .17oz.

BORSALINO fragrance by Borsalino Profumi. Milan, Italy. Distributed by The Wilkes Group, Inc. 4.5ml .15oz. The dark amber bottle has a "B" on the bottom.

BURBERRYS eau de toilette for men by Burberrys. Distributed by Royal Brands Int'l. NY, NY. 5ml .17oz.

CACHAREL eau de toilette pour homme by
Parfums Cacharel. Paris, France. 7.5ml 1/4oz.

Le 3e homme by Parfums Caron. Distributed by
Jean Patou, Inc. Paris, France. A Pochet et du
Courval Bottle.

PIERRE CARDIN men's cologne by Pierre
Cardin. Paris, France. Distributed by Jacqueline
Cochran. NY, NY. 3ml .1oz.

MUST eau de toilette, de Cartier, Inc. Paris,
France. 4ml .13oz. An oriental fragrance.

PASHA eau de toilette for men, de Cartier, Inc. Paris, France. 5ml .16oz.

EGOISTE eau de toilette pour homme by Chanel, Inc. Paris, France. 4ml .13oz.

ANTAEUS pour homme eau de toilette by Chanel, Inc. Paris, France. 4ml .13oz. A chypre fragrance. The black bottle has "CBG" on the bottom.

CARLO CORINTO eau de toilette pour homme by Parfums Carlo Corinto. Paris, France. A beautiful sculpted 10ml .33oz. bottle.

ENRICO COVERI eau de toilette pour homme by Enrico Coveri, Euroitialia. Monza, Italy. 6ml .2oz.

EAU SAUVAGE eau de toilette for men by Christian Dior Perfumes, Inc. Paris, France. A classic citrus fragrance in a diagonally fluted 10ml .33oz. bottle.

GIANFRANCO FERRE eau de toilette for men by Gianfranco Ferre, Diana De Silva Cosmetics. Cormano, Italy. Distributed by Gary Farn. Milford, CT. 5ml 1/6oz.

FAHRENHEIT eau de toilette for men by Christian Dior Perfumes, Inc. NY, NY. and Paris, France. 10ml .34oz. The ruby glass bottle has "PB1" on the bottom.

V.I.P. SPECIAL RESERVE extraordinary splash cologne for men by Giorgio Beverly Hills. Beverly Hills, CA. A chypre fragrance. 3.5ml 1/8oz.

XERYUS eau de toilette for men by Parfums Givenchy, Inc. Paris, France. 4ml .13oz.

GIVENCHY GENTLEMAN eau de toilette for men by Parfums Givenchy S.A. Paris, France. The clear glass 3ml .1oz. bottle is by Pochet et du Courval.

GUCCI NOBILE eau de toilette for men by Parfums Gucci. Distributed by Colonia, Inc. Paris, France. Distributed by Scannon Ltd., NY, NY. 5ml .17oz.

HERITAGE eau de toilette pour homme de
Guerlain, Inc. Paris, France. 4ml .13oz.

GUCCI pour homme by Gucci. Distributed by
Colonia, Inc. Paris, France. Distributed by
Scannon Ltd., NY, NY. 7.5ml 1/4oz.

HABIT ROUGE and VETIVER eau de toilette
pour homme de Guerlain. Paris, France.
4ml .13oz.

EQUIPAGE aftershave by Parfums Hermes. Paris, France. 10ml .3oz. "HERMES" is on the bottom of the bottle.

KRIZIA UOMO eau de toilette for men by Krizia Profumi. Milan, Italy. 5ml .16oz. A woody aromatic fragrance.

SERGIO SOLDANO eau de toilette for men by Intercosma Distributors. Genova, Italy. 5ml .18oz. A black, plastic-encased bottle with gold lettering.

LAGERFELD cologne by Parfums Lagerfeld. Distributed by Parfums Int'l. Ltd. Paris, France. 5ml .17oz.

ZINO DAVIDOFF eau de toilette for men by Davidoff Fragrances A.G. Zug. Distributed by Lancaster Group. NY, NY. Approx. 1/6oz.

DAVIDOFF COOL WATER eau de toilette for men. Distributed by Lancaster Group. NY, NY. Approximately 1/8oz.

LAPIDUS eau de toilette pour homme by Parfums Ted Lapidus. Paris, France. Distributed by The Fragrance Group, Ltd. One clear bottle and one grey bottle. 4ml .13oz.

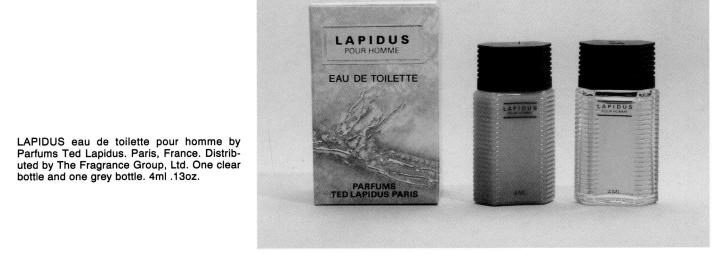

DRAKKAR NOIR eau de toilette for men by
Parfums Guy Laroche. Paris, France. The 5ml
.17oz. bottle is a Guy Laroche design. Distributed by Cosmair, Inc. NY, NY. A woody,
aromatic fragrance.

LEONARD fragrance pour homme by Leonard.
Distributed by Jean Pax, Inc. Paris, France.
Approximately 4ml.

POLO eau de toilette for men by Parfums Ralph
Lauren. Distributed by Cosmair, Inc. NY, NY.
A chypre fragrance in a 7ml bottle.

ESENCIA eau de toilette pour homme by Loewe.
Madrid, Barcelona, Londres, Spain. Approximately 1/4oz. "LOEWE" is on the bottom of the
bottle.

TABAC Original eau de toilette super concentrated for men by Maurer & Wirtz. West Germany. 4ml .13oz.

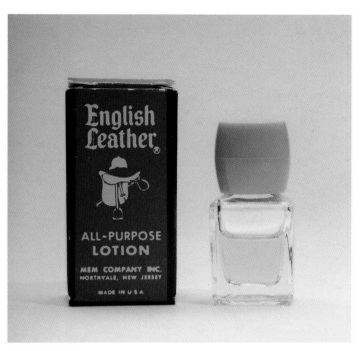

ENGLISH LEATHER all-purpose lotion for men by Mem Co., Inc. Northvale, NJ. 4ml .13oz. No label or markings.

CALIFORNIA cologne for men by Max Factor and Co., Hunt Valley, MD. A division of Proctor & Gamble. 3ml .1oz.

GATSBY eau de toilette pour lui by Pacoma Parfumeur, Paris, France. 4ml 1/8oz. A circled "P" is on the bottom of the bottle.

QUORUM eau de toilette for men by Antonio Puig. Barcelona, Paris and NY. The 7ml .02oz. bottle has a "C" on the bottom and holds a chypre fragrance..

FRANCESCO SMALTO eau de toilette for men by Francesco. Distributed by Parlux S A. Paris, France. 5ml .17oz.

SYBARIS eau de toilette for men by Puig. Paris, France. Distributed by Compar, Inc. 10ml .3oz. "SYBARIS" appears on the front of the glass.

SAMBA fragrance for men by The Perfumer's
Workshop, Ltd. NY, NY. 15ml .5oz. "SAMBA" is
on the bottom of the bottle.

RICCI-CLUB eau de toilette spray for men by
Nina Ricci. Paris, France. 4ml .14oz.

FRENCH LINE eau de toilette pour homme by
Revillon. Paris, France. 5ml 1/6oz.

SIGNORICCI 2 eau de toilette pour homme by
Parfums Nina Ricci. Paris, France. 7ml 1/4oz.
A classic citrus fragrance.

L'HOMME eau de toilette for men by Roger & Gallet. Paris, France. 7ml .24oz. A Saint Gobain Desjonqueres bottle.

TACTICS eau de toilette for men by Shiseido Cosmetici. Milan, Italy. 10ml .3oz.

PAUL SEBASTIAN fine cologne by Paul Sebastian. Paris, France. Approximately 5ml .16oz. The Pochet et du Courval trademark is on the bottom of the bottle.

V.O. eau de toilette pour homme de Jean-Marc Sinan. Paris, France. 5ml .16oz. The "HP" trademark is on the bottle.

BOUCHERON pour homme eau de toilette by Boucheron. Distributed by Ultra Cosmetics. Paris, France. Campbell & Thiselton, U.S.A. 5ml .16oz. The "HP" trademark is on the bottle.

OSCAR de la RENTA eau de toilette pour lui by Parfums Stern. Paris, France. Distributed by Sanofi Beauty Products. NY, NY. 10ml 1/3oz. A chypre fragrance.

VAN CLEEF & ARPELS pour homme eau de toilette. Distributed by Anthea in France and Sanofi Beauty Products in NY, NY. 5ml .17oz.

ROYAL COPENHAGEN cologne for men by Swank Inc. With permission from Royal Copenhagen. Denmark. 7.5ml .25oz.

VERSACE eau de toilette l'homme by Versace Profumi. Milan, Italy. Distributed by Vepro U.S.A., Ltd. 3.5ml 1/8oz. A chypre fragrance.

WORTH eau de toilette pour homme by Worth. Paris, France. 7ml 1/4oz.

TOUJOURS MOI ("Always Me") parfum by Corday. Paris, France. The beautiful, clear glass bottle, designed by René Lalique, contained a copper-colored oriental fragrance. 10ml.

BOUQUET D'ORIENT Approximately 1/8oz.

INNOVATION. The clear glass bottle has a cast-bronze flower basket glued to the bottle, with "INNOVATION" underneath the basket. Approximately 1/4oz.

Needlepoint Rose, a gold-encased glass bottle with a needle-point red rose, covered with thin plastic. A screw-on cap. The approximately 1/16oz. bottle is 1-3/8 inches tall.

A thin, vertical, lined bottle with a bronze colored cap. Approximately .1oz. Unknown scent.

A gold-encased glass bottle with blue and white rhinestones in a circular pattern, over a molded rose pattern. The cap has a plastic dabber attached.

A black glass bottle with a round glass overlay, painted with a blue flower in the center. The metal cap has a plastic dabber attached. "Made in Austria" is molded into the back of the bottle. Approximately 5ml.

Square, glass bottle. The Pochet et du Courval bottle contains an unknown scent. "Made in France" is on the bottom. Approximately 1/2oz.

A pink rose bottle. This beautiful bottle has a diamond pattern with a dainty, opaque rose stopper. 3ml .1oz.

This gold-encased bottle has "Japan" on the back. Approximately 1/4oz.

This enameled, gold-cased bottle appears to be hand painted enamel. Approximately 1/4oz.

This heart-shaped bottle is marked "Made in Germany" on the bottom. Unknown fragrance. Approximately 5ml.

"Cibott 2." The hourglass bottle has "Cibott 2" molded into the bottom.

This horioizontally fluted bottle brings the ginger jar to mind. Unknown fragrance, approximately 1/2oz.

Bottle, by I. W. Rice. NY. The swirled glass bottle has a screw-on cap topped with flowers, beads, and rhinestones, and is marked on the bottom with the trade name "IRICE".

LI LI BERMUDA. An import by I.W. Rice. NY, NY.

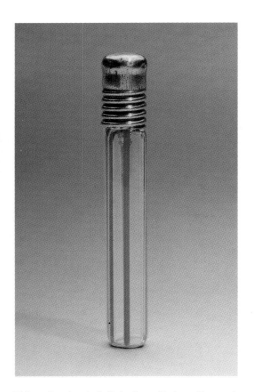

This red-striped vial is believed to be a Renaud, from Paris, France, and contained an unknown fragrance. The label is missing. Approximately 4ml. The bottle has "Made in Germany" etched in the glass. Brass cap and a glass dabber.

This silver-plate metal bottle is possibly of Asian origin. Approximately .2oz. The bottle is machined metal, silver plated. The metal dabber is 1-3/8 inches long and screws into the bottle. Gives the appearance of a vase with flowers.

A squat, round bottle, topped with an unusual amber-colored cap. Very quaint and pretty. Approximately 1/8oz.

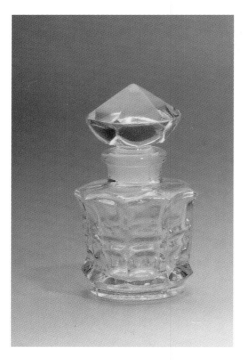

This bottle has a cut glass appearance and "Made in France" is on the bottom of the bottle. Approximately 1/4oz.

A snuffer. The cinnabar bottle is carved with oriental figures and scenery. The bottom has oriental writing and the stopper has a spoon-shaped dabber.

BLUE WALTZ perfume by Joubert. NY, NY. Approximately 1/4oz. The bottle's label is missing. "Made in USA" on the bottom.

This silver and pearl bottle has a covering of silver bows and a flowing pattern of embedded iridescent rhinestones and pretty pearls. Topped by a cap holding three small pearls. Approximately 1/4oz.

This square, pendant, gold-cased bottle has vertical cut vents and a screw type cap. Approximately 3ml.

This gold metal bottle for a charm bracelet has a screw cap with green and white rhinestones placed in a little flower pattern on the top. Approximately 1/16oz.

This pendant, heart-shaped, frosted glass bottle has "87 SANRIO" in gold letters and appears to have contained a pink liquid at one time. Approximately .13ml.

Both sides of this milk-glass pendant bottle are painted with flowers. The stopper has a small dabber.

These seven small, empty bottles contained unknown fragrances, but each is unique in its own design, even when unmarked.

ELEGANTE perfume by Avon Products, Inc. NY, NY. 1 dram. 1955-1959.

This snowflake bottle contains cologne by Avon Products Inc. NY, NY. 1/8oz. 1957-1958.

This dazzling bottle contains ELUSIVE by Avon Products Inc. NY, NY. 1/8oz. 1969-1974.

This swan bottle contains BIRD OF PARADISE perfume by Avon Products Inc. NY, NY. 1/8oz.

COTILLION and FOREVER SPRING fragrances by Avon Products Inc. NY, NY and Pasadena. Early 1950s.

CHARISMA perfume by Avon Products Inc. NY, NY. 1/8oz.

A snail bottle by Avon Products Inc. NY, NY. .25oz. 1968-1969.

The "Small Wonder Caterpillar" bottle with FIELD FLOWERS perfume, by Avon Products Inc. NY, NY. 1/8oz. 1972-1973.

The "Strawberry Fair" bottle with MOONWIND & SONNET perfumes by Avon Products Inc. \NY, NY. 1/8oz. 1974.

OCCUR! in an icicle perfume bottle by Avon Products Inc. NY, NY. 1 dram. 1967-1968.

The "Snow Man Petite" bottle with COTILLION perfume, by Avon Products Inc. NY, NY. .25oz. 1973.

The "Love Bird" bottle with CHARISMA perfume, by Avon Products Inc. NY, NY. .25oz. 1969-1970.

A pink flower bud bottle with ELUSIVE cologne, by Avon Products Inc. NY, NY. .5oz. 1969-1971.

UNFORGETTABLE cologne by Avon Products Inc. NY, NY. .5oz. 1970-1971.

A gold-capped rocker bottle with REGENCE cologne, by Avon Products Inc. NY, NY. .5oz. 1967-1968.

ELUSIVE PERFUME OIL by Avon Products
Inc. NY, NY. .5oz. 1969-1973.

PETITE PIGLET by Avon Products Inc. NY,
NY. 1/4oz. 1972.

A gingerbread house with SWEET HONESTY
cologne by Avon Products Inc. NY, NY. .5oz.
1983.

The "Precious Slipper" bottle with CHARISMA
perfume, by Avon Products Inc. NY, NY. .25oz.
1973-1974.

The "Perfume Petite Mouse" bottle with CHARISMA perfume, by Avon products Inc. NY, NY. .25oz. 1970.

A ladybug bottle with MOONWIND perfume, by Avon Products Inc. NY, NY. 1/8oz.

The "Dream Garden" bottle with BIRD OF PARADISE perfume oil by Avon Products Inc. NY, NY. 1972-1973.

The "Minuette" bottle with ELUSIVE cologne by Avon Products Inc. NY, NY. .5oz. 1969-1970.

A jewel bottle with TOPAZE perfume oil by Avon Products Inc. NY, NY. 5/8 dram. 1964-1965.

A flat-top rocker bottle with NEARNESS cologne, by Avon Products Inc. NY, NY. .5oz 1959-1962.

Estee Lauder's "Small Wonders" set,1991. By Estee Lauder, Inc. NY, NY. The set includes KNOWING parfum, .12oz., WHITE LINEN perfume, .09oz., SPELLBOUND perfume, .12oz., PRIVATE COLLECTION perfume, .07oz., and BEAUTIFUL perfume, .12oz.

"La Petite Collection" by Parfums Nina Ricci. Paris, France. 1992. The Petite Collection contains .11oz. Parfum Dove Flacon, .17oz. Parfum Purse Dove Flacon, .17oz. Eau de Parfum Opera Flacon, .2oz. Eau de Parfum Dove Flacon, .2oz. Eau de Toilette Romantic Flacon. The small flacons contain Nina Ricci's "L'AIR DU TEMPS" fragrance.

NINA RICCI
PARIS

L'Air du Temps

A display case containing many petite perfume
bottles available for collectors.

Perfume Information and Guidelines

Perfume is a volatile liquid that is distilled from flowers; it can also be prepared synthetically. Perfume contains more fragrance and oil than other scented preparations. Therefore, perfume has the highest fragrance strength value and the longest lasting effects, making it the most expensive of all preparations.

Cologne is a scented liquid consisting of a variety of fragrant oils in lesser amounts than in perfume, and contains more alcohol. It is also called *eau de cologne,* French for "cologne water." The word is derived from Koln (in French, Cologne), the city in western Germany where cologne has been made since the 18th century. The original cologne, 4711, is named after the street address of the parfum house that manufactured it in Koln, Germany.

Toilet water is a scented liquid with a high alcohol content, and is used in bathing, after shaving, or as a skin freshener.

FRAGRANCE STRENGTH

The strength values of fragrances in order of the highest to the lowest:
1. Parfum or perfume
2. Eau de parfum
3. Parfum de toilette
4. Eau de toilette
5. Eau de cologne
6. Cologne
7. Toilet water

FRAGRANCE ABBREVIATIONS

PARF=parfum
PERF=perfume
EDP=eau de parfum
PDT=parfum de toilette
EDT=eau de toilette
EDC=eau de cologne
COL=cologne
TW=toilet water

METRIC CONVERSION TABLE EQUIVALENTS OF COMMON PERFUME BOTTLES:

1.87 milliliters	= .0625 oz	= 1/16 oz	
3 ml	= .10 oz		
3.75 ml	= .125 oz	= 1/8 oz	= 1 dram
4 ml	= .13 oz		
5 ml	= .16 oz	= 1/6 oz	
6 ml	= .20 oz		
7.5 ml	= .25 oz	= 1/4 oz	
10 ml	= .333 oz	= 1/3 oz	
15 ml	= .5 oz	= 1/2 oz	
30 ml	= 1 oz		
60 ml	= 2 oz		

HELPFUL PERFUME TIPS

1. Keep fragrances out of extreme hot or cold temperatures. Cologne and toilet water can be kept in the refrigerator for a more lasting affect, but perfume should not be exposed to extreme hot or cold temperatures because it could affect the delicate balance.
2. When purchasing a new fragrance, take a coffee bean with you and sniff the coffee bean before smelling each new fragrance.
3. A lighter fragrance is best during warm months because heat intensifies a fragrance.
4. When choosing a new fragrance, wait till the fragrance dries before selecting it.
5. It is best not to try more than three scents at one time.
6. Never choose a fragrance because it smells good on someone else, everyone's body chemistry is different.
7. Apply your fragrance throughout the day to freshen the scent.
8. Build a wardrobe of fragrances for every occasion and mood.
9. Apply fragrances to the pulse points—wrists, inner elbows, throat and neck areas—for a lasting affect.

Fragrant Scents of Essence

Jasmine

Jasmine is a shrub or vine type plant of the genus *Jasminum*, mainly native to Asia. The flowers are either white or yellow and produce a fragrant scent called Jasmine, found in almost all perfumes.

Sandalwood

Sandalwood is a tropical Asian tree of the genus *Santalum*, having a yellowish hard wood used in carpentry. It produces an oil used in perfumery as a fixative to prevent rapid evaporation and to promote a long-lasting effect.

Henna

Henna is a tree or shrub of the genus *Lawsonia* from the Middle East. The flowers are white or reddish, and produce a strong perfume called Cyprinum. The leaves are dried and ground into a dye used in cosmetics.

Musk

Musk is one of the most powerful and sweet scents. For centuries the musk scent was made from the glandular secretions of the male musk deer found in central and northeast Asia. Today, musk is synthetically produced for practical reasons and remains a favorite scent for many.

Violet

The violet is a low-growing plant of the genus *Viola* and has been a favorite scent since the beginning of time. The method of extracting the perfume from the violet is a difficult and expensive process, therefore, most violet scents used in perfumery today are synthetic.

Patchouli

Patchouli is considered the strongest of all scents, therefore it is used in very small quantities. The small Asian shrub (*Pogostemon cablin*) is in the mint family, with the leaves producing a fragrant oil used in the manufacture of perfume.

Vetivert

Vetivert is a grass (*Vertivera zazaniodes*) from India. The grass has aromatic roots that yield an oil used in perfumery as a scent and a fixative.

Clove

An evergreen tree called *Syzygium aromaticum* produces these aromatic flower buds. Cloves are best known as a spice, but they were used to scent perfumes and oils in ancient times.

Castoreum

Castoreum is an odorous animal substance obtained from the groin glands of the beaver. At one time, it was used by perfumers as a fixative, but it is no longer popular with commercial perfume manufacturers for a number of reasons: supplies are short, prices are high, the methods of obtaining it are difficult, and the synthetics work just as well.

Ambergris

Ambergris is a waxy, gray substance formed in the intestines of the sperm whale, and is usually found floating at sea or washed ashore. It is used in perfumes as a scent and to slow down the evaporation rate. Since whaling almost caused the extinction of the sperm whale, commercial killing of whales has stopped, and a synthetic substitute has been produced.

Civet

Civet comes from the anal scent glands of the Civet cat of Africa and Asia. The thick, musky scented fluid is used in the manufacture of perfumes. Civet smells unpleasant in its raw state, but becomes pleasant when diluted and mixed with other scents. A synthetic substitute has been produced for practical reasons.

Lavender

Lavender consists of a variety of plants of the genus *Lavandula*, especially *L. angustifolia*. The plant produces clusters of small purplish flowers that produce a fragrant oil used in perfumery. Lavender is still a favorite scent today.

Frankincense

Frankincense is an aromatic gum resin obtained from trees of the genus *Boswellia* found in Africa and Asia. The gum resin is used as incense and in perfumes. At one time, Frankincense was one of the most valued substances in the ancient world of commerce, and was considered to be, above all else, a holy perfume.

Rose

The rose is considered the most popular of all flowers, consisting of a variety of shrubs or vines of the genus *Rosa*, with prickly stems and usually fragrant flowers. It is interesting to note that it takes over one thousand pounds of roses to obtain a single pound of rose essence. The fragrant oils obtained from the rose are considered the ultimate to the perfumer. The rose remains a favorite scent throughout the world.

The Art of Creating a Fragrance

The perfumer's job is to select and blend a wide variety of fragrant aromas into a new, pleasant, and successful perfume. The art of the creative perfumer requires experienced and skilled speculation, since there are no guarantees that mixing certain quanities of one aroma with certain quanities of another aroma will produce a pleasant smell. The perfumer is on his own, without detailed or precise formulas, and very few rules to follow when creating a new perfume. The perfumer is secretive about his formula and describes his product in general terms only; naturally he would not want his formula known. The perfumer is in a competitive business, so his perfume has to be different and difficult to copy.

The element of prediction is uncertain because the perfumer is dealing with immeasurables and intangibles, making the most precise blending of these tones of the fragrant mix very unpredictible. For example, attar of roses (attar is the fragrant oil or perfume obtained from flowers) is a common basic ingredient of a perfume. But there are many attars of roses, all different, because each type of rose smells different. No flower scent is a pure, single scent, but an intricate complexity of scents. The rose is a dominant scent, but there are overtones and undertones, so the blending of these tones make the perfume mix unpredictable.

The perfumer must produce a product that is different from his competitors' products. Certain qualities such as stability and staying power are achieved only by skillful mixing. Therefore, it is not just the task of extracting the perfume from the rose (for example), bottling it, and marketing it; the creative mixing skills of the perfumer must be called upon. Single scents by themselves are unlikely to be lasting best sellers; each ingredient has a powerful scent, some unpleasant when smelled individually. The perfumer is the mixer, with over five thousand materials available to work with. He may have an idea of the type of fragrance he wants to create, or he may not. Even for a perfumer experienced in his position, it is still skilled guesswork, for he cannot foresee that the outcome will produce a successful new fragrance. The process of creating a new perfume is time-consuming, and one fragrance can take years to perfect. A manufactured perfume may contain a mixture of over one hundred different fragrant substances, some natural and some artificial.

At his work, the perfumer is surrounded by many bottles, each containing different fragrances and oils. Even if he has a scent in mind for a new fragrance and knows what aromas he will use in blending, it is still time consuming. After the blending of each new addition, he dips small pieces of blotting paper into the mixture, lets them dry, then sniffs to see if he is getting close to his goal. Then the new fragrance must go through many tests to determine its lasting effect, for it is useless if the aroma changes under certain conditions, such as heat and humidity, and it must smell the same from morning to night. Most important, it must give off a consistent aroma for the life of the fragrance. Another important part of a perfume is the fixative, which gives the perfume its permanence, insuring that its varying ingredients do not evaporate at different rates, thus changing the original scent of the perfume. Each perfume needs a different type of fixative, and it must be chosen carefully, for a heavy fixative may overpower a delicate scent. Each fixative is an aromatic substance that will change the scent of the perfume like all the other ingredients.

Most perfumes on the market today, even the expensive ones, contain a large proportion of synthetic materials, partly because of the cost and availability of natural products. Synthetic aromatics fall into two groups, those that are copies of natural products, and those new scents that do not exist in nature. While synthetic materials are not necessarily cheaper products, they can be produced in large quantities, and they are more consistent and predictable than nature's scents. Although some traditionalists might argue that there is nothing like the real thing, it is not possible to say that a natural perfume is better than a synthetic one. CHANEL NO. 5 was the first sophisticated synthetic scent and has become an all-time classic in perfumery, blended by Ernst Beaux in 1923. Coty's L'AIMANT and Lanvin's ARPEGE followed within a few years, both using synthetics and both becoming classics. The methods of producing perfumes has changed remarkably since the revolution of the perfume industry in the last half of the 19th century, making perfumes more affordable. Today, new techniques in distillation and new materials such as synthetics have promoted the perfume industry into a successful world-wide market.

Bottle Designers and Manufacturers

Notable mention should be made of the skilled bottle designers and manufacturers for creating and producing all the beautiful perfume bottles. They have played an important role in the success of the perfume business and continue that role today. Glass is believed to date back to at least 3000 B.C., with the first glass container appearing from 1500 B.C. in Asia. But glass was probably experimented with in many areas of the world, not only in Asia. Although there are numerous great bottle designers and manufacturers, with all of them deserving recognition, I will only list a few, with no discredit intended for those not mentioned. As you collect the miniature fragrances, you will notice that most of the bottles produced are European, just as most of the fragrance trade is European. Some of the small bottles are produced by glassworks that have survived for centuries.

Many of the bottles will have the trademarks of the French companies. For example, "HP" is the trademark of Pochet et du Courval and "SGD" or "S" is the trademark of Saint Gobain Desjonqueres, etc. Most of the trademarks are found on the bottom of the bottles. Both of these companies have survived since the 1600s. Many of the bottles were designed by artists, while some bottle glassworks furnished their own designs. The first bottle factory in France was established in 1290.

The Pochet et du Courval Glass Company dates back to the1600s and probably makes most of the miniature perfume bottles that are on the market today. They make bottles for the fragrant scents by Balmain, Dior, Patou, and Cartier, to name a few. Their trademark is "HP/HP".

Saint Gobain Desjonqueres, dating from the 1600s, is also a large producer of modern perfume bottles today, making bottles for Balmain, Lancome, Roger and Gallet, and Gucci, etc. Their trademark is "SGD" or "S".

The Verreries Brosse Glass Firm, owned by E. Barre, designed and manufactured many scent bottles. Two popular names are APRIL SHOWERS by Cheramy and Coco Chanel's CHANEL NO. 5. Their trademark is "VB/BR".

Pierre Dinand is a very popular bottle designer. He designed beautiful and unique bottles for CARACTERE, K deKRIZIA, and YSATIS. The Dinand Workshop is a leading bottle maker today.

The Wheaton Glass Company is also a popular American glass factory that manufactures perfume bottles for American and European perfumers. They have also made bottles for Avon. EVENING IN PARIS, by Bourjois, is a popular bottle you can find today. Their trademark is "W" in a circle.

In the early 1900s, Francis Coty secured the talents of René Lalique to design commercial bottles for his scents and therefore revolutionized the scent trade. René Lalique also manufactured bottles with semi-automation, making perfume bottles more affordable. He continued in the glass business with much success, while he designed and manufactured bottles for Coty, Guerlain, and Molinard, etcetera. René Lalique's trademark is "RL" or "Lalique".

Marc Lalique, René's son, designed bottles for Jeanne Lancome, Raphael, Nina Ricci, Rochas, and many more. The firm is still controlled by the Lalique family.

The combination of Francis Coty and René Lalique's talents greatly changed the perfume industry, with Lalique's creations and reasonable prices of Coty's quality perfumes.

COLORS OF EARLY GLASS

It is interesting to note some of the early glass colors used in the scent bottle trade. There were many bright and vibrant colors, such as ruby red, amethyst, green, orange, gold topaz, violet blue, black, aqua, greenish amber, soft white opaque enamel, and cobalt blue (copper oxide).

These are just a few of the many beautiful colors that were created for perfume bottles. Terms such as "etching" or "flashing" on glass mean superimposing or laying a thin layer of colored glass upon clear glass. "Trailing" on glass gives a dripping effect. "Filigree" is the placement of rods with symetric designs in the glass, and "ice glass" has a cracked look. The chemical formula of glass consists of silica, alkaline flux and lime.

BOTTLE DESIGNERS

ANAIS ANAIS was created by Cheramy and the bottle design was by Annegrit Bier.
BEAUTIFUL was created by Estee Lauder and the bottle was designed by I. Levy-Alan Carre.
C'EST LA VIE! was created by Christian Lacroix and the bottle design was by Maurice Roger.
CALECHE was created by Hermes and the bottle design was by Joel Desgrippes.
DRAKKAR was created by Guy Laroche and the bottle was also designed by Guy Laroche.

JOY was created by Jean Patou and the bottle design was by Louis Sue.

LOU LOU was created by Cacharel and the bottle was by Annegret Bier.

PANTHERE was created by Cartier and the bottle was designed by Pochet et du Courval.

TAMANGO was created by Leonard and the bottle design was by Serge Mansau.

VANDERBILT was created by Gloria Vanderbilt and the bottle was designed by Bernard Kotyuk.

UNGARO was created Emanuel Ungaro and the bottle was designed by Jacques Helleu.

TRESOR was created by Lancome and the bottle design was by Areca.

JE REVIENS was created by Worth and the bottle design was by René Lalique.

LUCIEN LELONG was created by Nina Ricci and the bottle was designed by Marc Lalique.

FENDI was created by Parma and the bottle design was by Pierre Dinand.

SALVADOR DALI was created by S. Dali and the bottle design was also by Salvador Dali, with a likeness of his facial structure.

PALOMA PICASSO was created by Paloma, daughter of Pablo Picasso. Paloma also designed the bottle.

Coutures

Designer perfumes and fashionable wardrobes definitely go hand in hand. The perfume industry flourished in the nineteenth century and brought great potential for the coutures. Since high-fashioned clothes, accessories, and jewelry went well with perfume, the coutures invaded the scent market with their newly designed perfumes. They named perfumes after themselves and sold them in their shops to promote business. This added attraction in their shops proved very successful.

Many of the famous perfume companies of today entered the perfume business this way, many of which we can recognize today. The first is Coco Chanel, with her No. 5 perfume. Coco Chanel was also one of the first to have her expensive jewelry copied and introduced along with her clothing designs. The inexpensive reproductions became as much a part of fashion as the real thing. Thus the fashion world saw costume jewelry come into the picture. Many jewelry designers, along with the clothing designers, saw the opportunity to expand their business by capitalizing on their names in order to enter the scent market. Fashion designers looking for a sideline to promote business began to invade the scent market in the 1920s.

The established names of well-known fashion designers and jewelry designers are still recognized in the perfume industry today. Lanvin followed Chanel with ARPEGE, followed by Shiaparelli with SHOCKING, Balmain with VENT VERT and JOILE MADAME, Piquet with VISA and FRACAS, Marcel Rochas with FEMME, Balenciaga followed with FRUITE DES HEURES. Madame Gres had CABOCHARD, Dior followed with DIORRAMA, Patou's JOY and MOMENT SUPREME, Worth had DANS LA NUIT and JE REVIENS, and Saint Laurent's YSL was followed by RIVE GAUCHE. By the 1960s, most of the coutures had scents on the market that were very successful.

American fashion designers can also be identified in the perfume industry by their names, including Adolfo Sardina, Halston, Geoffrey Beene, James Galanos, Bill Blass, Calvin Klein, Oscar de la Renta, Anne Klein, Albert Nipon, Elizabeth Arden, and Norman Norell, just to name a few.

Well-known jewelry manufacturers are also recognized names in the perfume industry today. Louis Cartier, inventor of the wristwatch in 1907, is known in the perfume world, as is René Lalique, who designed jewelry and glass. Tiffany and Company has fragrances in addition to its exclusive jewelry line. Other famous names include Boucheron, Ciros, Gustave Faberge and Van Cleef and Arpels.

Avon

The California Perfume Company, known as Avon Products Incorporated today, was started in 1886 in New York City by David H. McConnel. The name of the business was unusual because the company was not located in California. The name of the company was suggested by a close friend who had visited California and was very impressed by the beautiful flowers there. Perfume was the only product being sold by the company at that time and "The California Perfume Company" transpired from the friend's suggestion. The company did very well from the beginning. The business grew, while more fragrances and other toiletry products were added. In 1895, a large new laboratory was built in Suffern, New York, and has been enlarged several times to accomodate the company's growth.

By 1915, the company was carrying a large line of products, such as perfumes, toilet articles and household products. The products were sold by CPC Representatives who went door to door, selling directly to the customer. The products were never sold in stores.

In 1929, a new line of cosmetics was introduced, called the Avon line. The new household line was named Perfection and given its own trademark. On the company's 50th Anniversary Year in 1936, the Good Housekeeping Seal of Approval was added to all Avon and Perfection products. All products since that time continue to bear the Seal of Approval.

Prior to 1936, the company steadily grew without doing any commercial advertising. Through 1936 and 1937, the company changed its policy on advertising during its 50th Golden Jubilee. Avon advertisements appeared in Good Housekeeping. The phrase "Avon Calling" became known all over the world. The California Perfume Company, which started in a one-room laboratory in New York City, has successfully grown into a world-wide network known as Avon Products Incorporated today.

The trend of collecting Avon bottles has become successful as well as enjoyable for bottle collectors through the years, and the interest is still strong today. The history of Avon can be found in the book "Avon Bottle Encyclopedia," written by Bud Hastin, which is very informative and interesting.

Bibliography

Carter, Ernestine. *The Changing World of Fashion.* New York, G.P. Putnam's Sons, First American edition 1977.

Hastin, Bud. *Avon Bottle Encyclopedia.* Written and produced by Bud Hastin. Missouri, Reliance Printing Co., 1974.

Heriteau, Jacqueline. *Potpurris and Other Fragrant Delights.* New York, Simon and Schuster, 1973.

North, Jacquelyne Y. Jones. *Commercial Perfume Bottles.* Pennsylvania, Schiffer Publishing, Ltd., 1987.

Poucher, W. A. *Perfumes, Cosmetics and Soaps.* Volume 1, "The Raw Materials of Perfumery." Revised by G. M. Howard. London, Chapman and Hall, Ltd., reprinted in 1976.

Poucher, W. A. *Perfumes, Cosmetics and Soaps.* Volume 2, "The Production, Manufacture and Application of Perfumes." London, Chapman and Hall, Ltd., 1976.

Trueman, John. *The Romantic Story of Scent.* London, Aldus Books Limited, 1975.

Winter, Ruth. *The Smell Book.* Philadelphia and New York, J. B. Lippincott Co., 1973.

List of Fragrances by House

Fragrance	Parfum House
"A" ANDIAMO	Princess Marcella Borchese
"A" ANNABELLA	R.P. Dennis
BOUQUET	Melillo Studios
"O" DE LANCOME	Parfums Lancome
VOTRE	Parfums Charles Jourdan
"Y"	Yves Saint Laurent
...WITH LOVE	Fred Hayman Beverly Hills
273	Fred Hayman Beverly Hills
'1000'	Jean Patou Inc.
4711	Colonia Inc.
A'BIENTOT	Lentheric
ACTION	Trussardi Parfums
ADDED ATTRACTION	Prince Matchabelli
ADOLFO	Francis Denney
ADOLFO CLASSIC GENTLEMEN	Adolfo Frag.Inc.
ALBARO	Aymone De Albaro
ALBERT NIPON	Albert Nipon Fragrance Inc.
ALLIAGE	Estee Lauder Inc.
AMARIGE	Parfums Givenchy Inc.
AMAZONE	Hermes
AMBERGRIS OIL	Alyssa Ashley
ANAIS ANAIS	Parfums Cacharel
ANIMALE	Parlux Fragrances Inc.
ANNE KLEIN	Parfums Anne Klein
ANNE KLEIN II	Parfums Anne Klein
ANTAEUS FOR MEN	Chanel Inc.
ANTILOPE	Weil
APPLE BLOSSOM	Duvinne
APRIL SHOWERS	Cheramy
ARMANI PARFUMS	Giorgio Armani
AROMATICS ELIXIR	Clinique Laboratories Inc.
ARPEGE	Lanvin Parfums Inc.
ASPEN	Quintessence Inc.
AVIANCE NIGHT MUSK	Prince Matchabelli
AZZARO 9	Parfums Loris Azzaro
AZZARO FOR MEN	Parfums Loris Azzaro
BAGHARI	Robert Piguet
BAL A VERSAILLES	Jean Desprez
BALAHE	Leonard Parfums
BANDIT	Robert Piguet
BASIC BLACK	Charles Revson Inc.
BASILE	Profumi Basile
BAVARDAGE	Charieres
BEAUTIFUL	Estee Lauder Inc.
BELLODGIA	Parfums Caron
BELOVED	Prince Matchabelli
BEVERLY HILLS GLAMOUR PERFUME	Gale Hayman Bev. Hills
BIJAN	Bijan Fragrances
BILL BLASS	Charles Revson Inc.
BLUE GRASS	Elizabeth Arden Ltd.
BLUE MARINE	Parfums Pierre Cardin
BLUE WALTZ	Joubert
BOB MACKIE	Bob Mackie
BORSALINO for men	Borsalino Profumi
BOSS SPORT for men	Hugo Boss
BOTANICAL	Naturalistics
BOUCHERON	Ultra Cosmetics
BOUCHERON for men	Ultra Cosmetics
BRIGHT CARNATION	Fuller Brush Co.
BURBERRYS for men	Burberry
BYBLOS	Rivara
BYZANCE	Rochas
C'EST	Royal Ungary
C'EST LA VIE!	Christian Lacroix
CABOCHARD	Parfums Gres
CACHAREL for men	Parfums Cacharel
CAESARS WOMAN	Caesars World Merchandising Inc.
CAFÉ	Café
CALANDRE	Paco Rabanne
CALECHE	Hermes
CALIFORNIA for men	Max Factor & Co.
CALYX	Prescriptives
CAMP BEVERLY HILLS	Colonia Inc.
CAPUCCI	Parfums Capucci
CARLO CORINTO for men	Parfums Carlo Corinto
CAROLINA HERRERA	Carolina Herrera Perfumes
CASMIR	Parfums Chopard
CASSINI	Oleg Cassini
CHANEL NO. 19	Chanel Inc.
CHANEL NO. 5	Chanel Inc.
CHANSON D'AMOUR	Jacques Bernier Inc.
CHANTILLY	Parfums Parquet
CHER UNINHIBITED	Parfums Stern
CHEVAL BLEU	Charles V
CHIYAT	Parfums Lancome
CHLOE NARCISSE	Parfums Int. Ltd.
CHLOÉ	Parfums Karl Lagerfeld
CIAO	Houbigant.
CIARA	Charles Revson
CLANDESTINE	Parfums Guy Laroche
COCO	Chanel Inc.
COLOGNE	Eau de Colonia Inc.
COLORS	Benetton Cosmetics Inc.
COLORS for men	Benetton Cosmetics Inc.
CONCRETA	Parfums Molinard
CORIANDRE	Jean Couturier
COURREGES IN BLUE	Courreges Parfums
CREATION	Parfums Ted Lapidus
CREATURE	Parfums Giles Cantuel
CRISTALLE	Chanel Inc.
CROYANCE	Charles V
DANGER	Parfums Ciro
DANIEL DE FASSON	Daniel Aubusson
DANS LA NUIT	Parfums Worth
DAVIDOFF COOL WATER for men	Lancaster Group
DECADENCE	Deco Dist. Group Inc.
DENEUVE	Parfums Stern
DESTINY	Marilyn Miglin Inc.

DETCHEMA	Parfums Revillon
DEVASTATING	Anjou
DILYS	Laura Ashley
DIORESSENCE	Christian Dior Perfumes
DIORISSIMO	Christian Dior Perfumes
DIVA	Parfums Ungaro
DRAKKAR NOIR for men	Parfums Guy Laroche
DUNE	Parfums Christian Dior
EAU DE GIVENCHY	Parfums Givenchy Inc.
EAU DE GUCCI	Gucci
EAU SAUVAGE for men	Christian Dior Perfumes
ECHO	Fox Fragrances
EGOISTE for men	Chanel Inc.
ELAN	Coty Inc.
EMERAUDE	Coty Inc.
ENCORE	Alfred Sung
ENGLISH LEATHER	
for men	Mem Co.
ENJOLI	Charles of the Ritz
ENRICO COVERI for men	Enrico Coveri
ENTENDU	Charles V
EQUIPAGE for men	Hermes
ESCADA	Escada Beaute
ESCAPE	Calvin Klein Cos. Co.
ESENCIA for men	Loewe
EVENING IN PARIS	Bourjois
EVENING STAR	Blanchard
FAHRENHEIT for men	Christian Dior Perfumes
FEMME	Rochas
FENDI	Parma Parfums
FIDJI	Parfums Guy Laroche
FIRST	Van Cleef & Arpels
FLEUR DE BOA	Parfums Boa
FLEURS D'ORLANE	Orlane
FLEURS DE ROCAILLE	Parfums Caron
FOREVER KRYSTLE	Carrington Parfums
FRACAS	Robert Piguet
FRANCESCO SMALTO	
for men	Parlux Fragrances Inc.
FRENCH LINE for men	Parfums Revillon
GALANOS	Parfums Galanos
GALIMARO NO. 5	Galimaro Parfumeur
GARDENIA	Ivel
GATSBY for men	Pacoma Parfumer
GEM	Van Cleef & Arpels
GENNY	Rivara
GIANFRANCO FERRE	Diana De Silva Cosmetiques
GIANFRANCO FERRE	
for men	Diana De Silva Cosmetiques
GIANNI VERSACE	Versace Profumi
GILDA	Pierre Wulff
GIORGIO	Giorgio Beverly Hills
GIVENCHY GENTLEMAN	Parfums Givenchy Inc.
GIVENCHY III	Parfums Givenchy Inc.
GLORIOUS	Gloria Vanderbilt
GOLDEN AUTUMN	Prince Matchabelli
GOLDEN DROP	Arcad'Elysse
GRAFFITI	Parfums Capucci
GUCCI 1	Gucci
GUCCI NO. 1	Gucci
GUCCI NO. 3	Gucci
GUCCI NOBILE for men	Gucci
GUCCI POUR HOMME	
for men	Gucci
GUESS	Fashion & Designer Fragrance Group Inc.
HABIT ROUGE for men	Guerlain
HALSTON COUTURE	Halston Fragrances
HERITAGE for men	Guerlain
HERMES	Hermes
HISTOIRE D'AMOUR	Daniel Aubusson
HOT	Charles Revson Inc.
ICEBERG	Iceberg Parfum
INCOGNITO	Noxell Corp.
INFINI	Parfums Caron
INTERLUDE	Francis Denney

INTIMATE	Revlon Inc.
INTRIGUE	Blanchard
ISADORA	Parfums Caron
IVORIE	Parfums Balmain
J'AIOSE	Parfums Guy Laroche
JACLYN SMITH'S	
CALIFORNIA	Procter & Gamble
JAGUAR for men	AlfinInc.
JE REVIENS	Parfums Worth
JEALOUSY	Blanchard
JIL SANDER for men	Jil Sander Cosmetics
JIL SANDER NO. 4	Jil Sander Cosmetics
JITROIS	Parfums Jean-Claude Jitrois
JMC	Jessica McClintock
JOLIE MADAME	Parfums Balmain
JONTUE	Revlon Inc.
JOOP!	Parfums Joop!
JOVAN MUSK	Jovan Inc.
JOY	Jean Patou Inc.
K DE KRIZIA	Krizia
KENZO	Kenzo
KL	Parfums Karl Lagerfeld
KNOWING	Estee Lauder Inc.
KRAZY KRIZIA	Krizia
KRIZIA UOMO for men	Krizia
L DE LOEWE	Loewe
L'AIMANT	Coty Inc.
L'AIR DU TEMPS	Nina Ricci
L'HOMME for men	Roger & Gallet
L'INSOLENT	Parfums Charles Jourdan
L'INTERDIT	Parfums Givenchy Inc.
L'ORIGAN	Coty Inc.
LA NUIT	Paco Rabanne
LAPERLA	Morris
LADY DI	Daver
LADY STETSON	Coty Inc.
LAGERFELD for men	Parfums Karl Lagerfeld
LAPIDUS for men	Parfums Ted Lapidus
LAUREN	Ralph Lauren
LE 3E for men	Parfums Caron
LE BYOU NUIT	Belafonte Int.
LE DE	Parfums Givenchy Inc.
LE JARDIN EXTRAIT	Max Factor
LE JARDIN FLEUR	
DE ROSE	Max Factor
LILY OF THE VALLEY	Fuller Brush Co.
LISTEN	Herp Alpert & Co. Inc.
LIZ CLAIBORNE	Liz Claiborne Cosmetics Inc.
LOU LOU	Parfums Cacharel
LUMIERE	Rochas
LUNA MYSTIQUE	Prince Matchabelli Inc.
LUTECE	Parfums Parquet
MA LIBERTE	Jean Patou Inc.
MACASSAR	Rochas
MADAME ROCHAS	Rochas
MADEMOISELLE RICCI	Nina Ricci
MAGIE NOIRE	Parfums Lancome
MAI TAI	Royal Hawaiian Per. Ltd.
MAISSA	Parfums Jean Louis Vermeil
MAJA	Myrugia
MALICA	Charles V
MAROC	Charles Revson
MAROC ULTIMA II	Revlon Inc.
MAXIM'S DE PARIS	Maxim's
MCM	MCM Cosmetic
METAL	Paco Rabanne
MICHELLE	Balenciaga
MISS DIOR	Christian Dior Perfumes
MISSONI	Missoni Profumi
MOLINARD DE MOLINARD	Parfums Molinard
MOMENTS	Priscilla Presley
MON CLASSIQUE	Morabito Parfums
MONOGRAM	Ralph Lauren
MONTAGE	Countess Maritza
MONTANA	Prestige Fragrances Ltd.
MOODS	Krizia

MOON SONG	Vanda Beauty Consultant
MOSCHINO	Herp Alpert & Co. Inc.
MUSK	Alyssa Ashley
MUST	Cartier Inc.
MUST for men	Cartier Inc.
MY SIN	Lanvin Parfums Inc.
NAJ-OLEARI	Euroitalia
NAVY	Noxell Corp.
NEW WEST Skin Scent	Aramis
NIKI DE SAINT PHALLE	Jacqueline Cochran
NINA	Nina Ricci
No. 3	Park & Tilford
NOCTURNES	Parfums Caron
NORELL	Prestige Fragrances Ltd.
NUDE	Charles Revson Inc.
OBSESSION	Calvin Klein Cos. Co.
OLIVIA	Deborah International Beauty Ltd.
OMAR	667 Perfumes Inc.
OMAR SHARIF	Parfums Omar Sharif
OMBRE BLEUE	Jean-Charles Brosseau
OMBRE ROSE	Jean-Charles Brosseau
ONLY	Mas Cosmetics
OPIUM	Yves Saint Laurent
OR NOIR	Morabito Parfums
ORANGE BLOSSOM	Howard Tawes
ORIENT	Charrier
OSCAR DE LA RENTA	Parfums Stern
OSCAR DE LA RENTA POUR LUI for men	Parfums Stern
PALOMA PICASSO	Parfums Paloma Picasso
PANTHERE	Cartier Inc.
PARADIS	Saks Fifth Avenue
PARFUM D'ETE	Kenzo
PARFUM RARE	Parfums Jacomo
PARFUM SACRE	Parfums Caron
PARIS	Yves Saint Laurent
PASHA for men	Cartier Inc.
PASSION	Parfums Int. Ltd.
PAUL SEBASTIAN for men	Paul Sebastian
PAVLOVA 1922	Parfums Payot
PERRY ELLIS	Parfums Stern
PIERRE CARDIN for men	Parfums Pierre Cardin
PIQUETTE	Pierre Vivion
PLATINE	Dana Perfumes Corp.
POISON	Christian Dior Perfumes
POLO FOR MEN	Ralph Lauren
PRESENSE	Parfums Parquet
PRIVATE COLLECTION	Estee Lauder Inc.
PRIVILEGE	Edmond Rosens
PROMESSE	Max Factor
PROPHECY	Prince Matchabelli
QUELQUES FLEURS L'ORIGINAL	Houbigant
QUORUM for men	Antonio Puig
RAFINEE	Houbigant
RARE JEWEL	Countess Maritza
REALITIES	Liz Claiborne Cosmetics Inc.
RED	Giorgio Beverly Hills
RED DOOR	Elizabeth Arden Ltd.
REGINE'S	Parfums Regine's
REPLIQUE	Raphael
RICCI-CLUB for men	Nina Ricci
RIVE GAUCHE	Yves Saint Laurent
ROMA	Laura Biagiotti
ROMEO	Romeo Gigli
ROSE CARDIN	Parfums Pierre Cardin
ROYAL COPENHAGEN for men	Swank Inc.
ROYAL SECRET	Lancaster Group
RUFFLES	Oscar De La Renta
RUMBA	Balenciaga
SAFARI	Ralph Lauren
SALVADOR DALI	Parfums Salvador Dali
SAMBA	The Perfumers Workshop Ltd.
SAMBA for men	The Perfumers Workshop Ltd.

SAMSARA	Guerlain
SAND & SABLE	Coty Inc.
SCAASI	Prestige Fragrances Ltd.
SCHERRER 2	Parfums Jean-Louis Scherrer
SCOUNDREL	Revlon Inc.
SEA SPLASH	Naturalistics
SECRET DE VENUS ZIBELINE	Weil
SENSO	Parfums Ungaro
SERGIO SOLDANO for men	Intercosma
SHABANITA DE MOLINARD	Parfums Molinard
SHALIMAR	Guerlain
SHOCKING	Schiaparelli
SIGNORICCI 2 for men	Nina Ricci
SILENCES	Parfums Jacomo
SILENT NIGHT	Countess Maritza
SINAN	Jean-Marc Sinan
SIROCCO	Lucien Lelong
SKIN MUSK	Bonnie Bell
SOCIETY	Royal Brands Int'l.
SONATA	J.S. Bach
SPECTACULAR	Parlux Ltd.
SPELLBOUND	Estee Lauder Inc.
SUNG	Alfred Sung
SWANN	Pacoma Parfumer
SYBARIS for men	Puig
TABAC for men	Maurer & Wirtz
TABAC BLOND	Parfums Caron
TABU	Dana Perfumes Corp.
TACTICS for men	Shiseido Cosmetici
TAMANGO DE LEONARD	Leonard Parfums
TATIANA	Diane Von Furstenberg Inc.
TEA ROSE	The Perfumers Workshop Ltd.
TEATRO ALLA SCALA	Krizia
TEMPORA	A Blanc
TIFFANY	Tiffany & Co.
TIGRESS	Parfums Faberge
TITA	Tita Rossi
TOUJOURS MOI	Corday
TRESOR	Parfums Lancome
TROPICS	Naturalistics
TUSCANY for men	Aramis
UN JOUR	Parfums Charles Jourdan
UNGARO	Parfums Ungaro
V.I.P. for men	Giorgio Beverly Hills
V.O. for men	Jean-Marc Sinan
VALENTINO	Parfums Stern
VAN CLEEF & ARPELS for men	Van Cleef & Arpels
VANDERBILT	Gloria Vanderbilt
VE VERSACE	Versace Profumi
VENDETTA	Valentino
VENT VERT	Parfums Balmain
VERSACE for men	Versace Profumi
VETIVER	Guerlain
VEUX TU	Charrier
VISA	Robert Piguet
VIVARA	Emilio Pucci
VOICE	Christian de Lenclos
VOLUPTE BY OSCAR DE LA RENTA	Parfums Stern
WEIL DE WEIL	Weil
WIND SONG	Prince Matchabelli Inc.
WHITE DIAMONDS	Parfums Int. Ltd.
WHITE LINEN	Estee Lauder Inc.
WHITE SHOULDERS	Parfums Int. Ltd.
WOODHUE	Parfums Faberge
WORTH for men	Parfums Worth
XERYUS for men	Parfums Givenchy Inc.
YOUTH DEW	Estee Lauder Inc.
YSATIS	Parfums Givenchy Inc.
ZEENAT	Parfums Zeenat Aman
ZIG ZAG	Zsa Zsa
ZINO DAVIDOFF for men	Lancaster Group

List of Manufacturers and Fragrances

Parfum House	Fragrance
Adolpho Fragrances, Inc.	ADOLPHO CLASSIC GENTLEMEN for men
Alfin, Inc.	JAGUAR for men
Herp Albert & Co., Inc.	LISTEN
Herp Albert & Co., Inc.	MOSCHINO
Albaro	ALBARO, AYMONE DE
Parfums Zeenat Aman	ZEENAT
Anjou	DEVASTATING
Aramis	NEW WEST SKIN SCENT
Aramis	TUSCANY for men
Arcad'Elysse	GOLDEN DROP
Elizabeth Arden, Ltd.	BLUE GRASS
Elizabeth Arden, Ltd.	RED DOOR
Parfums Giorgio Armani	ARMANI
Alyssa Ashley	AMBERGRIS OIL
Alyssa Ashley	MUSK
Laura Ashley	DILYS
Parfums Daniel Aubusson	DANIEL DE FASSON
Parfums Daniel Aubusson	HISTOIRE D'AMOUR
Parfums Loris Azzaro	AZZARO for men
Parfums Loris Azzaro	AZZARO 9
J. S. Bach	SONATA
Balenciaga	LE DIX
Balenciaga	MICHELLE
Balenciaga	RUMBA
Parfums Balmain	IVORIE
Parfums Balmain	JOLIE MADAME
Parfums Balmain	VENT VERT
Profumi Basile	BASILE
Belafonte Int.	LE BYOU NUIT
Bonnie Bell, Inc.	SKIN MUSK
Benetton Cosmetics, Inc.	COLORS
Benetton Cosmetics., Inc.	COLORS for men
Jacques Bernier, Inc.	CHANSON D'AMOUR
Laura Biagotti	ROMA
Bijan Fragrances, Inc.	BIJAN
A Blanc	TEMPORA
Blanchard	EVENING STAR
Blanchard	INTRIGUE
Blanchard	JEALOUSY
Parfums Boa	FLEUR DE BOA
Princess Marcella Borchese	"A" ANDIAMO
Borsalino Profumi	BORSALINO for men
Hugo Boss	BOSS SPORT for men
Bourjois	EVENING IN PARIS
Jean-Charles Brosseau	OMBRE BLEUE
Jean-Charles Brosseau	OMBRE ROSE
Burberrys	BURBERRYS for men
Parfums Cacharel	ANAIS ANAIS
Parfums Cacharel	CACHAREL for men
Parfums Cacharel	LOU LOU
Caesars World Merchandising	CAESARS WOMAN
Café	CAFÉ
Parfums Giles Cantuel	CREATURE
Parfums Capucci	CAPUCCI
Parfums Capucci	GRAFFITI
Parfums Pierre Cardin	BLUE MARINE
Parfums Pierre Cardin	PIERRE CARDIN for men
Parfums Pierre Cardin	ROSE CARDIN
Parfums Caron	BELLODGIA
Parfums Caron	FLEURS DE ROCAILLE
Parfums Caron	INFINITI
Parfums Caron	ISADORA
Parfums Caron	LE 3E for men
Parfums Caron	NOCTURNES
Parfums Caron	PARFUM SACRE
Parfums Caron	TABAC BLOND
Cartier, Inc.	MUST
Cartier, Inc.	MUST for men
Cartier, Inc.	PANTHERE
Cartier, Inc.	PASHA for men
Carrington Parfums	FOREVER KRYSTLE
Oleg Cassini	CASSINI
Chanel, Inc.	ANTAEUS for men
Chanel, Inc.	CHANEL NO. 5
Chanel, Inc.	CHANEL NO. 19
Chanel, Inc.	COCO
Chanel, Inc.	CRISTALLE
Chanel, Inc.	EGOISTE for men
Charieres	BAVARDAGE
Charles of the Ritz	ENJOLI
Charles V.	CHEVAL BLEU
Charles V.	CROYANCE
Charles V.	ENTENDU
Charles V.	MAJICA
Charrier	ORIENT
Charrier	VEUX TU
Cheramy	APRIL SHOWERS
Parfums Chopard	CASMIR
Parfums Ciro	DANGER
Liz Claiborne Cosmetics, Inc.	LIZ CLAIBORNE
Liz Claiborne Cosmetics, Inc.	REALITIES
Clinique Laboratories, Inc.	AROMATICS ELIXER
Jacqueline Cochran	NIKI DE SAINT PHALLE
Corday	TOUJOURS MOI
Colonia, Inc.	4711
Colonia, Inc.	COLOGNE, EAU DE
Colonia, Inc.	CAMP BEVERLY HILLS
Parfums Carlo Corinto	CARLO CORINTO for men
Coty, Inc.	ELAN
Coty, Inc.	EMERAUDE
Coty, Inc.	L'AIMANT
Coty, Inc.	L'ORIGAN
Coty, Inc.	LADY STETSON
Coty, Inc.	SAND & SABLE
Countess Maritza	MONTAGE
Countess Maritza	RARE JEWEL
Countess Maritza	SILENT NIGHT
Courreges Parfums	COURREGES IN BLUE
Jean Couturier	CORIANDRE
Enrico Coveri	ENRICO COVERI for men
Parfums Salvador Dali	SALVADOR DALI
Dana Parfums Corp.	PLATINE
Dana Parfums Corp.	TABU

Daver	LADY DI
Deborah International Beauty, Ltd.	OLIVIA
Deco Dist. Group, Inc.	DECADENCE
Francis Denney	ADOLFO
Francis Denney	INTERLUDE
R. P. Dennis	"A"
Jean Desprez	BAL a VERSAILLES
Diana De Silva Cosmetiques	GIANFRANCO FERRE
Diana De Silva Cosmetiques	GIANFRANCO FERRE for men
Christian Dlor Perfumes	DIORESSENCE
Christian Dior Perfumes	DIORISSIMO
Christian Dior Perfumes	DUNE
Christian Dior Perfumes	EAU SAUVAGE for men
Christian Dior Perfumes	FAHRENHEIT for men
Christian Dior Perfumes	MISS DIOR
Christian Dior Perfumes	POISON
Duvinne	APPLE BLOSSOM
Escada Beaute	ESCADA
Euroitalia	NAJ-OLEARI
Parfums Faberge	TIGRESS
Parfums Faberge	WOODHUE
Max Factor	CALIFORNIA for men
Max Factor	LE JARDIN EXTRAIT
Max Factor	LE JARDIN FLEUR DE ROSE
Max Factor	PROMESSE
Fashion & Designer Frag. Group, Inc.	GUESS
Fox Fragrances	ECHO
Fuller Brush Co.	BRIGHT CARNATION
Fuller Brush Co.	LILY OF THE VALLEY
Diane Von Furstenberg, Inc.	TATIANA
Parfums Galanos	GALANOS
Galimaro Parfumeur	GALIMARO No. 5
Giorgio Beverly Hills	GIORGIO
Giorgio Beverly Hills	RED
Giorgio Beverly Hills	V. I. P. for men
Parfums Givenchy, Inc.	AMARIGE
Parfums Givenchy, Inc.	EAU DE GIVENCHY
Parfums Givenchy, Inc.	GIVENCHY III
Parfums Givenchy, Inc.	GIVENCHY GENTLEMEN for men
Parfums Givenchy, Inc.	L'INTERDIT
Parfums Givenchy, Inc.	LE DE
Parfums Givench, Inc.	XERYUS for men
Parfums Givenchy, Inc.	YSATIS
Parfums Gres	CABOCHARD
Gucci	EAU de GUCCI
Gucci	GUCCI 1
Gucci	GUCCI NO. 1
Gucci	GUCCI NO. 3
Gucci	GUCCI NOBILE for men
Gucci	GUCCI POUR HOMME for men
Guerlain	HABIT ROUGE for men
Guerlain	HERITAGE for men
Guerlain	SAMSARA
Guerlain	SHALIMAR
Guerlain	VETIVER
Halston Fragrances	HALSTON COUTURE
Fred Hayman Beverly Hills	273
Fred Hayman Beverly Hills	...WITH LOVE
Gale Hayman Beverly Hills	BEVERLY HILLS GLAMOUR PERFUME
Hermes	AMAZONE
Hermes	CALECHE
Hermes	EQUIPAGE for men
Hermes	HERMES
Carolina Herrera Perfumes	CAROLINA HERRERA
Houbigant	CIAO
Houbigant	QUELQUES FLEURS L'ORIGINAL
Houbigant	RAFINEE
Intercosma	SERGIO SOLDANO for men
Iceberg Perfume	ICEBERG
Ivel	GARDENIA
Parfums Jacomo	PARFUM RARE
Parfums Jacomo	SILENCES
Jil Sander Cosmetics	JIL SANDER for men
Jil Sander Cosmetics	JIL SANDER NO. 4
Parfums Jean-Claude Jitrois	JITROIS
Joubert	BLUE WALTZ
Parfums Charles Jourdan	L'INSOLENT
Parfums Charles Jourdan	UN JOUR
Parfums Charles Jourdan	"VOTRE"
Jovan, Inc.	JOVAN MUSK
Parfums Joop!	JOOP!
Kenzo	KENZO
Kenzo	PARFUM D'ETE
Parfums Anne Klein	ANNE KLEIN
Parfums Anne Klein	ANNE KLEIN II
Calvin Klein Cosmetics Co.	ESCAPE
Calvin Kelin Cosmetics Co.	OBSESSION
Krizia	K de KRIZIA
Krizia	KRAZY KRIZIA
Krizia	KRIZIA UOMO for men
Krizia	MOODS
Krizia	TEATRO ALLA SCALA
Christian Lacroix	C'EST LA VIE!
Parfums Karl Lagerfeld	CHLOÉ
Parfums Karl Lagerfeld	KL
Parfums Karl Lagerfeld	LAGERFELD for men
Lancaster Group	DAVIDOFF COOL WATER for men
Lancaster Group	ROYAL SECRET
Lancaster Group	ZINO DAVIDOFF for men
Parfums Lancome	CHIYAT
Parfums Lancome	MAGIE NOIRE
Parfums Lancome	"O" DE LANCOME
Parfums Lancome	TRESOR
Lanvin Parfums, Inc.	ARPEGE
Lanvin Parfums, Inc.	MY SIN
Parfums Ted Lapidus	CREATION
Parfums Ted Lapidus	LAPIDUS for men
Parfums Guy Laroche	CLANDESTINE
Parfums Guy Laroche	DRAKKAR NOIR for men
Parfums Guy Laroche	FIDJI
Parfums Guy Laroche	J'AIOSE
Estee Lauder, Inc.	ALLIAGE
Estee Lauder, Inc.	BEAUTIFUL
Estee Lauder, Inc.	KNOWING
Estee Lauder, Inc.	PRIVATE COLLECTION
Estee Lauder, Inc.	SPELLBOUND
Estee Lauder, Inc.	WHITE LINEN
Estee Lauder, Inc.	YOUTH DEW
Ralph Lauren	LAUREN
Ralph Lauren	MONOGRAM
Ralph Lauren	POLO for men
Ralph Lauren	SAFARI
Lucien Lelong	SIROCCO
Christian de Lenclos	VOICE
Lentheric	A'BIENTOT
Leonard Parfums	BALAHE
Leonard Parfums	TAMANGO DE LEONARD
Loewe	ESENCIA for men
Loewe	L DE LOEWE
Bob Mackie	BOB MACKIE
Mas Cosmetics	ONLY
Maurer & Wirtz	TABAC for men
Maxim's	MAXIM'S DE PARIS
MCM Cosmetic	MCM
Jessica McClintock	JMC
Milillo Studios	"BOUQUET"
Mem Co.	ENGLISH LEATHER for men
Marilyn Miglin, Inc.	DESTINY
Missoni Profumi	MISSONI
Parfums Molinard	CONCRETA
Parfums Molinard	HABANITA DE MOLINARD
Parfums Molinard	MOLINARD DE MOLINARD
Morabito Parfums	MON CLASSIQUES
Morabito Parfums	OR NOIR
Morris	LAPERLA
Myrugia	MAJA
Naturalistics	BOTANICAL
Naturalistics	SEA SPLASH
Naturalistics	TROPICS
Albert Nipon Fragrance, Inc.	ALBERT NIPON

Noxell Corp.	INCOGNITO
Noxell Corp.	NAVY
Parfums Omar Sharif	OMAR SHARIF
Orlane	FLEURS D'ORLANE
Oscar De La Renta	RUFFLES
Paco Rabanne	CALANDRE
Paco Rabanne	LA NUIT
Paco Rabanne	METAL
Pacoma Parfumer	GATSBY for men
Pacoma Parfumer	SWANN
Parfums Int. Ltd.	CHLOE NARCISSE
Parfums Int. Ltd.	PASSION
Parfums Int. Ltd.	VENDETTA BY VALENTINO
Parfums Int. Ltd.	WHITE DIAMONDS
Parfums Int. Ltd.	WHITE SHOULDERS
Parfums Parquet	CHANTILLY
Parfums Parquet	LUTECE
Parfums Parquet	PRESENCE
Park & Tilford	No. 3
Parlux Fragrances, Inc.	ANIMALE
Parlux Fragrances, Inc.	FRANCESCO SMALTO for men
Parlux, Ltd.	SPECTACULAR
Parma Parfums, Int'l	FENDI
Jean Patou, Inc.	'1000'
Jean Patou, Inc.	JOY
Jean Patou, Inc.	MA LIBERTE
Parfums Payot	PAVLOVA 1922
The Perfumers Workshop, Ltd.	SAMBA
The Perfumers Workshop, Ltd.	SAMBA for men
The Perfumers Workshop, Ltd.	TEA ROSE
Parfums Paloma Picasso	PALOMA PICASSO
Robert Piguet	BAGHARI
Robert Piguet	BANDIT
Robert Piguet	FRACAS
Robert Piguet	VISA
Prescriptives	CALYX
Priscilla Presley	MOMENTS
Prestige Fragrances, Ltd.	MONTANA
Prestige Fragrances, Ltd.	NORELL
Prestige Fragrances, Ltd.	SCAASI
Prince Matchabelli	AVIANCE NIGHT MUSK
Prince Matchabelli	ADDED ATTRACTION
Prince Matchabelli	BELOVED
Prince Matchabelli	GOLDEN AUTUMN
Prince Matchabelli	LUNA MYSTIQUE
Prince Matchabelli	PROPHECY
Prince Matchabelli	WIND SONG
Procter & Gamble	JACLYN SMITH'S CALIFORNIA
Emilio Pucci	VIVARA
Puig	QUORUM for men
Puig	SYBARIS for men
Quintessence, Inc.	ASPEN
Parfums Regine's	REGINE'S
Raphael	REPLIQUE
Parfums Revillon	DETCHEMA
Parfums Revillon	FRENCH LINE for men
Revlon, Inc.	INTIMATE
Revlon, Inc.	JONTUE
Revlon, Inc.	MAROC ULTIMA II
Revlon, Inc.	SCOUNDREL
Charles Revson	BASIC BLACK
Charles Revson	BILL BLASS
Charles Revson	CIARA
Charles Revson	HOT
Charles Revson	MAROC
Charles Revson	NUDE
Nina Ricci	L'AIR DU TEMPS
Nina Ricci	MADEMOISELLE RICCI

Nina Ricci	NINA
Nina Ricci	RICCI-CLUB for men
Nina Ricci	SIGNORICCI 2 for men
Rivara	BYBLOS
Rivara	GENNY
Rochas	BYZANCE
Rochas	FEMME
Rochas	LUMIERE
Rochas	MACASSAR
Rochas	MADAME ROCHAS
Roger & Gallet	L'HOMME for men
Romeo Gigli	ROMEO
Edmond Rosens	PRIVILEGE
Tita Rossi	TITA
Royal Brands, Int'l.	SOCIETY
Royal Hawaiian Perfume, Ltd.	MAI TAI
Royal Ungary	C'EST
Saks Fifth Avenue	PARADIS
Parfumes Jean-Louis Scherrer	SCHERRER 2
Schiaparelli	SHOCKING
Paul Sebastian	PAUL SEBASTIAN for men
Shiseido Cosmetici	TACTICS
Jean-Marc Sinan	SINAN
Jean-Marc Sinan	V. O. for men
Parfums Stern	DENEUVE
Parfums Stern	PERRY ELLIS
Parfums Stern	OSCAR DE LA RENTA
Parfums Stern	OSCAR DE LA RENTA POUR LUI for men
Parfums Stern	OSCAR DE LA RENTA'S RUFFLES
Parfums Stern	CHER UNINHIBITED
Parfums Stern	VALENTINO
Parfums Stern	VOLUPTE BY OSCAR DE LA RENTA
Alfred Sung	ENCORE
Alfred Sung	SUNG
Swank Inc.	ROYAL COPENHAGEN for men
Howard Tawes	ORANGE BLOSSOM
Tiffany & Co.	TIFFANY
Trussardi Parfums	ACTION
Ultra Cosmetics	BOUCHERON
Ultra Cosmetics	BOUCHERON for men
Parfums Ungaro	DIVA
Parfums Ungaro	SENSO
Parfums Ungaro	UNGARO
Van Cleef & Arpels	FIRST
Van Cleef & Arpels	GEM
Van Cleef & Arpels	VAN CLEEF & ARPELS for men
Vanda Beauty Consultant	MOON SONG
Gloria Vanderbilt	GLORIOUS
Gloria Vanderbilt	VANDERBILT
Parfums Jean Louis Vermeil	MAISSA
Versace Profumi	GIANNI VERSACE
Versace Profumi	VE VERSACE
Versace Profumi	VERSACE for men
Pierre Vivion	PIQUETTE
Weil	ANTILOPE
Weil	SECRET DE VENUS ZIBELINE
Weil	WEIL DE WEIL
Parfums Worth	DANS LA NUIT
Parfums Worth	JE REVIENS
Parfums Worth	WORTH for men
Pierre Wulff	GILDA
Yves Saint Laurent	OPIUM
Yves Saint Laurent	PARIS
Yves Saint Laurent	RIVE GAUCHE
Yves Saint Laurent	"Y"
Zsa Zsa	ZIG ZAG
667 Perfumes, Inc.	OMAR

Price Guide

This price reference is intended to be a guide only. Because the marketplace is constantly changing, prices may be lower or higher than stated herein. These prices have been found in the geographical area to which the author has access. Many factors determine the price, including the size and condition of the bottle, whether the bottle is full or empty, and if the fragrance has its original box.

Fragrance	Bottle Size	Price (U.S. $)
"A" Andiamo	1/4oz	5
"A" Annabella	.17oz	7
"Bouquet"	.13oz	5
"L'Air du Temps" Dove Flacon		16
"L'Air du Temps" Lalique	1/9oz	11
"L'Air du Temps" Opera Flacon and funnel in case		75
"L'Air du Temps" Opera Flacon		15
"L'Air du Temps" Purse Dove		15
"L'Air du Temps" Romantic Flacon in dome		18
"O" de Lancome	.25oz	9
"Votre"	1/15oz	8
"Y"	.13oz	9
"Y"	.26oz	9
'1000'	.07oz	10
...With Love	1/8oz	16
273 Rodeo Drive	1/8oz	17
A'Bientot	.13oz	8
Action	mini	6
Added Attraction Red Crown	1 dram	15
Adolfo Classic Gent for men	1/2oz	5
Adolfo	.13oz	10
Adolfo col	.33oz	10
Albaro	.17oz	7
Albert Nipon	1/8oz	11
Alliage	.1oz	12
Amarige	1/8oz	10
Amazone	.23oz	7
Ambergris Oil	.48oz	5
Anais Anais	.3oz	11
Animale	.17oz	13
Anne Klein	1/8oz	10
Anne Klein II	1/8oz	7
Antaeus pour homme	.13oz	7
Antilope	1/8oz	5
Apple Blossom	1/8oz	7
April Showers	1/8oz	10
Armani	.16oz	10
Armani pour homme	.33oz	5
Aromatics Elixir		8
Arpege	1/4oz	5
Aspen	3/8oz	10
Aviance Night Musk	.25oz	10
Azzaro 9	.17oz	4
Azzaro pour homme	.24oz	6
Baghari	1/16oz	5
Bal A Versailles	.08oz	9
Balahe	1/8oz	6
Bandit	.13oz	7
Basic Black rep., Hot rep., Nude rep.	1/8oz	5 each
Basile	.17oz	17
Bavardage	1/16oz	5
Beautiful	.12oz	16
Bellodgia, Fleurs de Rocaille, Noct., T. Blond	set	20
Beverly Hills	.1oz	12
Bijan	.25oz	18
Bill Blass replica	1/8oz	8
Blue Grass	.5oz	11
Blue Marine	.14oz	6
Bob Mackie	1/8oz	6
Borsalino	.15oz	5
Boss Sport	.17oz	6
Botanical, Sea Splash, Tropics	.17oz	5 each
Boucheron	.17oz	16
Boucheron pour homme	.16oz	8
Burberrys for men	.17oz	12
Byblos	.25oz	13
Byzance	.1oz	7
C'est	1/16oz	5
C'est La Vie!	.13oz	20
Cabochard	.06oz	8
Cacharel pour homme	1/4oz	10
Caesars Woman	1/8oz	5
Café	.13oz	5
Calandre	.17oz	6
Caleche	1/4oz	8
California for men	.1oz	5
Calyx	.18oz	10
Camp Beverly Hills	.5oz	10
Capucci	1/6oz	11
Carlo Corinto pour homme	.33oz	8
Carolina Herrera	.13oz	10
Casmir	.17oz	14
Cassini	.125oz	8
Chanel No. 19	.2oz	11
Chanel No. 5	1/3oz	100
Chanel No. 5	1/4oz	75
Chanel No. 5 edp	.14oz	15
Chanel No. 5 edt	.14oz	11
Chanel No. 5, gold cap		11
Chanel No. 5, round stopper		25
Chanson D'Amour	.5oz	5
Chantilly	.12oz	6
Cher Uninhibited edt	1/3oz	12
Cher Uninhibited parf	1/8oz	16
Cheval Bleu	1/16oz	5
Chiyat de Lancome	1/16oz	7
Chloe Narcisse	1/8oz	16
Chloé	.11oz	10
Ciao	1/8oz	8
Ciara	1/8oz	14
Clandestine	.16oz	8
Coco	.13oz	8
Colors	.13oz	5
Colors for men	.13oz	5
Concreta	1 dram	10
Coriandre	.3oz	11
Courreges In Blue	.2oz	10
Creation	.13oz	5
Creature	.15oz	11
Cristalle	.2oz	13
Croyance	1/16oz	5
Danger	1.25 drams	10
Daniel De Fassion	1/8oz	10
Dans La Nuit	.22oz	11
Davidoff Cool Water for men	1/8oz	5
Decadence	.16oz	13
Deneuve	1/8oz	12
Destiny	1/8oz	13
Detchema	1/8oz	11
Devastating	1/2oz	5
Dilys	.1oz	12
Dioressence edt	.34oz	11
Diorissimo edt	.34oz	11
Diva	.14oz	11
Drakkar Noir for men	.17oz	12
Dune	.17oz	17
Eau de Givenchy	1/8oz	5
Eau de Gucci	.25oz	6
Eau Sauvage for men	.33oz	7
Echo	.17oz	10
Egoiste pour homme	.13oz	7
Elan	.5oz	7
Emeraude	.125oz	10
Emeraude	.25oz	10
Emeraude & L'Aimant, gold cased	.13oz	15 each
Encore	.14oz	15
English Leather for men	.13oz	5
Enjoli	1/8oz	5
Enrico Coveri pour homme	.2oz	5
Entendu	1/16oz	5
Equipage for men	.3oz	11
Escada	.14oz	13
Escape	.13oz	25
Esencia pour homme	1/4oz	7
Evening In Paris	.5oz, 15, 25oz	10 each
Evening In Paris	.64 dram	5
Evening In Paris	1 dram & .5oz	10 each
Evening Star, Intrigue, Jealousy	1.25 dram	5 each
Evening Star Parfum Traveler	1/8oz	15
Fabergette Woodhue	1 dram	10
Fahrenheit for men	.34oz	11
Femme	.1oz	7
Fendi	.16oz	13
Fidji	.16oz	10
Fidji	1/16oz	5
First	.17oz	8
Fleur de Boa	.23oz	11
Fleurs D'Orlane	.16oz	7
Forever Krystle	.25oz	8
4711	.17oz	5
Fracas	.13oz	7
Francesco Smalto for men	.17oz	5
French Line pour homme	1/6oz	8
Galanos	.25oz	5
Galimaro No. 5	1/2oz	5
Gardenia by Ivel	1/4oz	8
Gatsby pour lui	1/8oz	5
Gem	.17oz	6
Genny	.17oz	8
Gianfranco Ferre	1/6oz	10
Gianfranco Ferre for men	1/6oz	9
Gianni Versace	1/8oz	9
Gilda	1/6oz	8
Giorgio Beverly Hills Parf	.11oz	16
Giorgio RED Perf	1/8oz	20
Givenchy Gent for men	.1oz	6
Givenchy III	1/8oz	6
Glorious	.13oz	8
Golden Autumn	.5 dram	5
Golden Drop	1/8oz	6
Graffiti	1/16oz	5
Gucci No. 3	1/8oz	6
Gucci Nobile for men	.17oz	6
Gucci Parfum 1	1.25oz	5
Gucci pour homme	1/4oz	5
Guess	.12oz	10
Habanita	1/4oz	10
Habit Rouge pour homme	.13oz	9
Halston Couture	1/8oz	11
Heritage pour homme	.13oz	17
Hermes	.25oz	11
Histoire D'Amour	.14oz	7
Houbigant gold case	.25oz	15
Iceberg	.17oz	12
Incognito	.1oz	5
Infini	1/4oz	5
Interlude	1/8oz	5
Intimate	.25oz	12
Intimate purse flacon	.1oz	15
Isadora	1/8oz	8
Ivorie	.25oz	9
j'aiOse	.11oz	11
Jaclyn Smith's California	.3oz	5
Jaguar for men	.17oz	12
Je Reviens	1/8oz	10
Jil Sander No. 4	.17oz	15
Jitrois	.2oz	13
JMC	1/4oz	8
Jolie Madame	1/16oz	7
Jontue	.2oz	20
Joop!	.1oz	10
Jovan Musk	1/8oz	6
Joy	.07oz	10
K de Krizia	.13oz	6
Kenzo	1/8oz	11
KL	1/3oz	10
Knowing	.12oz	16

Name	Size	Price
Krazy Krizia	.2oz	14
Krizia uomo	.16oz	5
L de Loewe	1/6oz	9
L'Homme for men	.24oz	7
L'Insolent	.125oz	8
L'Interdit	1/8oz	9
L'Origan	1/8oz	10
La Nuit	.17oz	10
Lady Di	1/16oz	6
Lady Stetson	3/8oz	7
Lagerfeld col	.17oz	10
LaPerla	1/4oz	12
Lapidus pour homme	.13oz	5
Lauren	1/4oz	11
Le 3e homme	mini	5
Le Byou Nuit	1/2oz	9
Le De	1/16oz	5
Le Dix	.1oz	6
Le Jardin Extrait, Le Jardin Fleur de Rose	.12oz	5 each
Leonard pour homme	.13oz	5
Lily of the Valley, Bright Carnation	1 dram	7 each
Listen	.125oz	11
Liz Claiborne	1/8oz	13
Lou Lou	.17oz	8
Lumiere	.1oz	8
Luna Mystique	.25oz	5
Lutece	.12oz	6
Ma Liberte	.2oz	11
Macassar	.17oz	8
Madame Rochas	.1oz	9
Mademoiselle Ricci	.16oz	11
Magie Noire	.25oz	10
Mai Tai	1/2oz	5
Maissa	.23oz	7
Maja	.25oz	8
Malica	1/16oz	5
Maroc	1/8oz	10
Maroc Ultima II	1/3oz	8
Maxim's	.14oz	5
Maxim's	1/3oz	8
MCM	.17oz	8
Metal	.17oz	8
Michelle	.16oz	7
Miss Dior edt	.34oz	11
Missoni	1/8oz	11
Molinard	1/4oz	10
Moments	.08oz	5
Mon Classique	1/8oz	8
Monogram	1/4oz	5
Montage, Rare Jewel, Silent Night set	.25oz	5 each
Montana	.07oz	10
Moods	.2oz	11
Moon Song	.13oz	5
Moschino	1/8oz	8
Musk by Alyssa Ashley	.13oz	7
Must Black	.13oz	11
Must Red	.13oz	10
My Sin	.25oz	12
My Sin	1oz	12
Naj-Oleari	.16oz	11
Navy	.1oz	5
New West	.25oz	10
Niki de Saint Phalle	.20oz	9
Nina	1/2oz	10
No. 3 Park & Tilford	.1oz	5
Nocturnes	.16oz	7
Nocturnes	.25oz	30
Norell	1/8oz	17
Obsession	.12oz	20
Olivia	.5oz	5
Omar 667	1/4oz	5
Omar Sharif	1/4oz	5
Ombre Bleue	.16oz	10
Ombre Rose	.16oz	6
Only	.3oz	11
Opium	.1oz	14
Or Noir	1/7oz	11
Orange Blossom	1/2oz	5
Orient	1/16oz	5
Oscar de la Renta Parf	mini	13
Oscar de la Renta pour lui	1/3oz	11
Paloma Picasso	1/8oz	9
Paloma Picasso	gold case	5
Panthere	.13oz	24
Paradis	.25oz	5
Parfum D'Ete	.17oz	23
Parfum Rare	1/6oz	8
Parfum Sacre	.1oz	25
Paris parf	.26oz	12
Pasha for men	.16oz	16
Passion	1/8oz	15
Paul Sebastian for men	.16oz	5
Pavlova 1922	.06oz	6
Perry Ellis	.14oz	11
Pierre Cardin man's col	.1oz	8
Piquette	1/2oz	15
Platine	1/8oz	7
Poison	.17oz	17
Polo for men	.2oz	12
Presense	.12oz	6
Private Collection	.09oz	16
Privilege	.13oz	8
Promesse	.1oz	5
Prophecy	1 dram	7
Quelques Fleurs L'Original	.1oz	12
Quorum for men	.02oz	5
Raffinee	.25oz	12
Raffinee	1/8oz	12
Realities	.17oz	17
Red Door	.25oz	11
Regine's	.17oz	8
Replique	1/16oz	5
Ricci-Club for men	.14oz	6
Rive Gauche	.1oz	10
Roma	.17oz	9
Romeo	.25oz	12
Rose Cardin	.25oz	12
Royal Copenhagen for men	.25oz	5
Royal Secret	.25oz	8
Ruffles	.13oz	10
Ruffles	.17oz	10
Rumba	.13oz	9
Safari	1/8oz	18
Salvador Dali	.17oz	10 each
Samba	1/4oz	5
Samba for men	.5oz	5
Samsara	.07oz	19
Sand & Sable	.25oz	7
Scaasi	1/8oz	20
Scherrer 2	1/8oz	6
Scoundrel	.3oz	5
Secret de Venus Zibeline	.22oz	14
Senso	.1oz	10
Sergio Soldano for men	.18oz	7
Shalimar	.07oz	25
Shalimar	1/2oz	100
Shalimar	.07oz	25
Shalimar	1oz	200
Shalimar	1/16oz	12
Shocking dress form	.13oz	10
Signoricci 2 pour homme	1/4oz	8
Silences	1/16oz	6
Sinan edt	.16oz	8
Sinan parf	1/8oz	12
Sirocco	.25oz	7
Skin Musk	1/8oz	5
Skin Oil, Korean		8
Society	.14oz	12
Sonata	.25oz	12
Spectacular	.17oz	5
Spellbound	.12oz	16
Sung	.14oz	13
Swann	1/8oz	5
Sybaris for men	.3oz	14
Tabac for men	.13oz	5
Tabu	1/4oz	5
Tabu	1/8oz	5
Tactics for men	.3oz	11
Tamango	.13oz	8
Tatiana col		5
Tea Rose	1/2oz	9
Tea Rose	1/6oz	6
Teatro alla Scala	1/8oz	7
Tempora	1/16oz	5
Tiffany	1/8oz	17
Tigress	1/4oz	25
Tita	.17oz	21
Tresor	.25oz	17
Tuscany for men	.25oz	5
Un Jour	.08oz	5
Ungaro	.1oz	11
V.I.P. for men	1/8oz	9
V.O. pour homme	.16oz	8
Valentino	1/4oz	5
Van Cleef & Arpels pour homme	.17oz	5
Vanderbilt edt	.22oz	10
Vanderbilt parf	1/8oz	16
Ve Versace	1/8oz	12
Vendetta	.25oz	10
Vent Vert	.13oz	11
Versace l'homme	1/8oz	10
Vetiver pour homme	.13oz	9
Veux Tu	1/16oz	5
Visa	4/5 dram plaid	15
Vivara	1/16oz	5
Voice	.17oz	8
Volupte	1/8oz	17
Weil de Weil	1/8oz	8
White Diamonds	1/8oz	18
White Linen	.09oz	16
White Shoulders	.25oz	13
Wind Song	.25oz	14
Worth pour homme	1/4oz	7
Xeryus for men	.13oz	6
Youth Dew	.25oz	10
Ysatis	1/8oz	8
Zeenat	.25oz	10
Zig Zag	1/4oz	5
Zino Davidoff for men	1/6oz	9

Index